CW00854215

HOW TO GET A JOB IN PR

SARAH STIMSON

First Published 2013

Edited by Caro Moses

www.unlimitedmedia.co.uk/caromoses

Formatted by Jo Harrison

www.writersblockauthorservices.co.uk

Cover by Ryan Ashcroft

www.loveyourcovers.com

ISBN: 978-1492944287

For my parents. Thank you.

My university education was not wasted after all.

"There has never been a more exciting time to work in public relations. This book is a must read guide to finding your first job. Sarah has helped countless people start out and develop their careers and now wants to help you."

Stephen Waddington, European Digital & Social Media Director at Ketchum & CIPR President 2014

"PR is on the up. While other industries shrank during the recession, PR grew, and grew strongly. Competition for that entry-level job is accordingly fierce -so if you want to break into PR, immerse yourself in this book. It's an investment you'll never regret."

Francis Ingham, Director General, PRCA

About the author

I live in a small seaside town in north Essex, with my long-suffering husband, son, two cats and a dog.

I have worked in recruitment and training in the PR industry for over a decade. During that time, I've placed people in jobs both in PR agencies and in-house communications teams, from entry level all the way up to the most senior PR roles. Most recently, I've concentrated on helping graduates enter the PR profession and in particular have worked as the Course Director for the Taylor Bennett Foundation, a charity dedicated to improving diversity in the industry.

So far, over 100 graduates have been through the Foundation's programme and I've advised them all on their job searches. I started looking around for a book to recommend to them, a "how to get a job" type book, but everything I found was either aimed at people already working, or were not specific enough for the PR industry. So, I decided to write one.

You can find me on Twitter: www.twitter.com/goooorooo

On Facebook: www.facebook.com/stimsonsarah

On LinkedIn: www.linkedin.com/in/stimsonsarah

On my blog: www.stimsonsarah.com

Or contact me by email: stimsonsarah@gmail.com

10% of the royalties from this book will be donated to the Taylor Bennett Foundation. You can read more about the Foundation's work, and make a donation if you'd like to, here: www.taylorbennettfoundation.org

Acknowledgements

In order to give a broad perspective on the industry, I asked lots of PR practitioners, both senior and junior, for their observations on entry-level jobs and how to go about getting one and keeping it. I also included comments from experienced PR lecturers, recruiters and headhunters.

I am extremely grateful for their thoughts, and my thanks go to the many brilliant contributors:

Elizabeth Adams, Iain Anderson, Michele Andjel, Leke Apena, Nina Arnott, Lawrence Atkinson, Bolu Babalola, Richard Bailey, Robert Bailhache, Brian Beech, Antonia Betts, Liz Birchall, Simon Brocklebank-Fowler, Jo Burkill, Di Burton, Victoria Brough, Tajah Brown, Whitney Brown, Liz Bridgen, Ian Burge, Matt Cartmell, Jonathan Charles, Jonathan Clare, Nick Clark, Gene Cleckley, Adam Clyne, Robert Cole, Simon Collister, Brendon Craigie, Jane Crofts, Seri Davies, Andraea Dawson-Shepherd, Mark Demery, Nick Ede, Jackie Elliot, Vernon Everitt, Jane Fletcher, Giles Fraser, David Gallagher, Nicola Gibb, Lorna Gozzard, Francis Graham, Lucie Harper, Neil Hedges, Julian Henry, Samantha Howard, Francis Ingham, Joe Jenkins, Avril Lee, John Lehal, Charles Lewington, Cat Macdonald, Ben Matthews, Simon Matthews, Steve McCool, Heather McGregor, Monique McKenzie, Dominic McMullan, Lekha Mohanlal, John Moorwood, Trevor Morris, Palissa Osei-Owusu, Alex Pearmain, Robert Phillips, Stewart Prosser, Chris Reed, Rebecca Salt, Philip Sheldrake, Paul Simpson, Donald Steel, Hilary Stepien, Gareth Thompson, Brigitte Trafford, Stephen Waddington, Andrew Walton, Faye Wenman, Toyosi Wilhelm, Steffan Williams, Philip Young.

I'd particularly like to thank Heather McGregor for encouraging me to write this book and for guiding me through the publishing process.

Thanks also to Caro Moses for her invaluable editorial support, Jo Harrison for her book design expertise, and Ryan Ashcroft for the fabulous cover art. I wholeheartedly recommend all three.

Finally, thanks to my husband Paul, who was patient and supportive as I withdrew from family life in order to finish writing. And to our son Franklin, who was not quite as patient.

Introduction

Youth unemployment figures are currently at record highs. If you're leaving school, college or university with hopes of embarking on a career, it may feel like a huge mountain to climb. For some entry-level job seekers, it's simply an issue of not knowing what options are accessible to them, which leads to little or no strategy in their job search.

The public relations industry is very much open to young job hunters; it's just a case of knowing what opportunities are available, and how to go about getting yourself noticed by an employer.

I've worked with a lot of very bright graduates in the last five years and they have had some striking similarities. Although some of them were aware that PR includes a range of disciplines and sectors, the vast majority of them were completely bowled over by the different areas of communications open to them. If you didn't know that internal communications, corporate communications, public affairs, celebrity PR and digital PR were all different branches of the same industry, then you're not alone.

They were also keen to enter the industry but were going the wrong way about it. In a competitive job market you should send out as many applications as possible, right? Well, that's true to an extent, but those applications need to be tailored for each job and each employer: scatter gunning generic CVs and cover letters will get you nowhere. I know you won't believe me, but when you've sent out fifty applications and had no replies then come back and read this book again.

Of course, it's all very well me telling them to tailor their CV, but if they don't know what kind of skills and experience PR employers value, then how do they know what is relevant information to include?

All of them were very aware that they needed relevant experience on their CV, but hardly any of them knew where to look for that experience or how to stand out from the crowd.

These are clever graduates. Most of them have been top of their class throughout school and university and yet, when it comes to breaking into the communications industry, they really struggled.

All this information is out there on blogs, PR company websites and industry publications and for those of us working in the industry it can be incredibly frustrating that young job seekers seem to ignore it all. Except that I suspect they aren't ignoring it, they just don't know it's there.

It is not by accident that many universities have ditched their careers departments and replaced them with employability teams. Educational institutions are starting to recognise that degrees may not be all that an employer wants, and giving their students and graduates skills that employers value is important if they want their alumni to succeed.

In this book I hope to gather together all the useful advice you will need to embark on a career in PR. Some of its content has already appeared on my blog and has been rewritten and put together in a sensible order. Much of it is completely new. You will learn about the practical steps you can take to getting a job in the communications industry and how to make yourself more employable. You can consider it your own employability department.

You don't just have to take my word for it, either. PR degrees are becoming increasingly popular, and are offered by a number of UK universities. The lecturers on those courses are well informed and many of them have experience of working in the communications industry so their opinions are very valid. Several of them have been kind enough to share their thoughts with you in this book. There are also lots of fantastic contributions from senior PR practitioners who have had long and illustrious careers; they recruit people just like you, so pay attention to what they say. I've also included comments from PRs who have been in the industry less than twelve months. Who better than people who have recently been through the job-hunting process to tell you how to do it?

Part 1: An overview of PR employment

Before you set about applying for jobs in PR, you should have a decent understanding of the industry and how it operates. The first part of this book should give you at least a basic understanding, but to really get a comprehensive view you should do some research too. Read the trade press, have a look at top communications consultancies' websites, and talk to people in the industry. Only then will you be able to make an informed decision about the types of job that might suit you, and tailor your applications appropriately.

The PR industry is incredibly competitive. Only top talent is making its way into the industry, and employers are choosy - very choosy - about who they let through their doors.

The good news is that most hires these days are made on merit, rather than who you are related to, but who you know still remains the quickest way to get a foot in the door and so networking is increasingly important.

It's also vital that when you apply for a job you know exactly what it is you're applying for, not least because you are bound to be asked about your motivation if you get to interview stage, so it's good to be clear about why you want to work for that company in particular, and in the industry in general. Identifying which part of the industry you'd be interested in, and suited to, is the first step in that process.

Chapter 1: What is PR?

What is PR? That should be a pretty simple question to answer. Except, it isn't. If you ask someone outside of the industry to give an example of a PR person they invariably pick one of the following three:

1) Edina from Absolutely Fabulous
2) Max Clifford
3) Alastair Campbell

Lots of PR practitioners would scoff at the first two of those examples (and a few might scoff at the last one too). Edina is fictional, obviously, but it's said that she's based on PR veteran Lynne Franks (yes, her off I'm a Celebrity Get Me Out of Here). The truth is, there are some PRs like that. Some call it 'fluffy bunny PR', implying there are no serious issues to deal with and that those PRs represent trivial clients – usually celebs of a Z list nature. But if you are a celebrity, even a Z list one, it is very feasible that you might need some PR support, and so a certain portion of the market is there to provide that service. They may not be all be the champagne guzzling dahhhlings that appeared in Ab Fab, but they do a job.

The debate rages on in the communications industry as to whether Max Clifford is a PR practitioner or a publicist (you may wonder if there is a difference and indeed, it's a thin line).

Alastair Campbell is another well-known personality in the PR industry and is revered by some and loathed by others. It is safe to say that he is respected, and he operates in an area of a communications some call government affairs and others call public affairs.

Hang on a minute, what happened to PR?

Ah, yes: PR isn't just PR. It covers a vast range of disciplines and sectors and the industry is ever expanding. So although I refer to PR or communications throughout this book, that covers a huge range of jobs. Let's start with sectors.

Imagine you are a huge pharmaceutical company. Some people hate you because you're making massive profits off the back of sick people who have no choice but to buy your drug. That could damage your reputation, right? So you definitely need someone in your PR department.

And that applies to any other contentious industry so oil, tobacco, fur, gambling, fast food – all the companies in those industries have PR departments.

But it's not just companies that have to deal with difficult issues and criticism that have communications teams. The vast majority of large corporations have PR people, and these days even small firms have them too. So PRs operate in industries as diverse as automotive, retail, publishing, charity, technology, beauty, music, financial services, professional services, arts and government.

There are three sectors in particular which may not be self-explanatory and it's worth me mentioning them here as you are bound to see them in job adverts and wonder what they are. The technology sector tends to be split into two halves; B2B tech and consumer tech. B2B means business to business, so if you're working in that sector you are likely to be dealing with PRing products which appeal to other businesses, e.g. computer chips or servers. Consumer tech is much more focussed on the end user of that product – the consumer – and so you're more likely to be PRing products like smartphones or MP3 players. "B2B" isn't exclusively used in the tech sector, and you may see it used to describe other jobs too; it might apply if you are PRing shop fitting products, for example.

Another sector that seems to confuse a lot of people is healthcare. Jobs in this sector tend to be advertised as OTC or ethical healthcare. OTC stands for over the counter and is also sometimes referred to as consumer healthcare. This sector is concerned with anything you would be able to buy in a chemist or pharmacist without a prescription, e.g., piles cream, ibuprofen, condoms, corn plasters etc.

Ethical healthcare is basically anything you'd need a prescription for. Drug therapies, chemotherapy, erectile dysfunction drugs, heart medications and so on.

Finally, you should be aware of the difference between financial services and financial PR. PRs working in financial services work for clients who deliver services in the financial sector – so retail banks and insurance companies for example. Financial PR is a discipline rather than a sector and you should be careful not to confuse the two.

Disciplines are the different types of PR within those sectors. These disciplines are many and varied and there seems to be new ones almost every year. PRs all over the country will be throwing their hands up in horror when they read my description of their discipline but I have tried to keep the explanations as simple as possible; just keep in mind that there are complexities in each discipline, so these short descriptions should just be your starting point and it's worth further investigation if any of them take your fancy.

Financial PR. When a company buys another company there will be a financial PR company in the background managing the communications around that acquisition. They are also on hand to give advice during mergers and IPOs (initial public offerings – when a company is first floated on a stock exchange).

Investor relations. Closely related to Financial PR, investor relations is what it says on the tin – managing the company's relationship with its investors, as opposed to its relationship with the media, which is what Financial PR is much more focussed on. There is often cross over between investor relations and financial PR.

Corporate communications. The easiest way to explain corporate communications is to think of it as PR for the company, rather than for a particular product.

Consumer PR. This is much more brand related. Consumer PR deals with PRing a particular product or service.

B2B PR. Business to business PR is communicating messages to other businesses who might buy your products, rather than direct to consumers.

Public affairs. These practitioners aim to engage government departments in order to influence public policy.

CSR. Corporate Social Responsibility, sometimes just called Social Responsibility or Sustainability is a business's way of operating in a socially responsible way. This may be through charitable donations, or by managing its impact on the environment, the local community and its employees.

Digital. Many PR practitioners would argue that Digital PR is no longer a separate discipline and should be integrated into your work whichever discipline you work in. However, jobs are still sometimes advertised as digital PR so it's worth you knowing what it is. Digital PR is concerned with online reputation – often using social media to build relationships.

Internal communications. As the title suggests, internal communications deals with communicating messages internally rather than externally. Sometimes it's called employee relations. It is very much a separate discipline from external communications/media relations, and practitioners tend to have very specific experience, although some people manage both external and internal communications.

Just to confuse you, sectors and disciplines are often interchangeable – healthcare PR, for example, is sometimes considered both a sector and a discipline.

So, back to Edina, Max and Alastair. They *are* examples of PR practitioners, but the industry is much, much broader than that, and you should consider all sectors and disciplines when thinking about what you would actually like to do.

To my mind, what PR boils down to is this: reputation management. Whether you are managing the reputation of a celebrity, an oil company, the latest smart phone, a political party, a charity, a supermarket, an online dating site or a book publisher, the skills required are essentially the same. The sector

8

is different and the discipline may be different but it all comes down to reputation.

"What is PR? This is a simple question that doesn't actually have a simple answer. The activities labelled PR come in a variety of shades and contexts, and actual practice depends on the practitioner's understanding and experience, the requirements and values of the practitioner's employer or client, and the norms and values of society.

A common manifestation could be described as publicity, activity designed solely to drive awareness and interest amongst those people who matter to the organisation's success – past, present and future customers for example. It can focus heavily on media relations to the point where some conflate media relations to be public relations.

Closely related to publicity, we have a form of practice frequently referred to as spin. This is a form of propaganda, an approach intent on interpreting events with bias, and perhaps disingenuously or manipulatively as needed. It's this type of activity that has tarnished PR's reputation, ironically.

At the other end of the spectrum is the form I subscribe to and champion. Often called the excellence model of PR, it entails the planned and sustained effort to influence opinion and behaviour, and to be influenced similarly, in order to build mutual understanding and goodwill. This dialogical practice is about growing relevance, reputation and trust. Unlike publicity, it is not a sub-discipline of marketing.

Social media and related technologies have impacted all forms of PR practice. Firstly, practitioners can now build relationships with publics directly as well as via intermediaries such as journalists. Secondly, some pundits consider social media to have brought about "radical transparency" – it's difficult, for example, to project a façade to the world whilst behaving quite differently in private when every single person is carrying around a high-definition video camera in their pockets!

"Perception is reality" is a common phrase, but perhaps this is being flipped round – reality is perception. Such technological and behavioural pressures might make spin more difficult and support the growth of the excellence model in practice. At least I certainly hope so."

Philip Sheldrake, Managing Partner, Euler Partners and author, The Business of Influence – reframing marketing and PR for the digital age (Wiley, 2011), and Attenzi – a social business story (2013), @sheldrake

"Many have tried to come up with a simple definition of PR and many have failed, principally because it's no single thing. On the one hand, it's not too difficult to guess the activities that PR entails. Namely, liaison with the media, explaining ideas to journalists, getting them interested in your client or employer's story or point of view. Then there's a great deal of demonstrating value as well; media evaluation and reporting are vital disciplines. On the other hand, PR is all the clichés you've ever heard: schmoozing clients and reporters, endless networking, capitalising on breaking news, sourcing random props for photo shoots (I once had to find a rugby ball in the City of London in less than three hours – a more difficult task than it sounds). And yes, being active on social media is pretty much obligatory these days. PR differs from sector to sector, and between agency and in-house, yet the basic tenets remain the same. If I were to boil PR down to two things, I'd say it's about opportunities and reputation. Finding opportunities for your clients or employer to achieve positive media coverage; and managing the situation on the occasions when negative coverage threatens to harm their reputation. Both of these cover a vast range of activities and responsibilities, but broadly speaking, they're the two areas I've expended the most energy on during my career."

Ian Burge, Senior Account Manager, Cognito, @IanBurgePR

"When I was young, I used to believe in a rational and objective world. As you age, you realise how unconnected things really are. PR aims to bridge that gap, connecting people and their organisations with the right ideas and conversations. Some see that as sinister. I'm a humanist, so I see it as helping people and organisations to express themselves in a way that gives them the greatest chance of being understood in what they mean."

Robert Bailhache, Director of Communications, Direct Line Group

"Good public relations is a business tool, not a nice-to-have fluffy extra. Good PR will ensure the strategy of an organisation, whether public, private, charitable or institutional, is properly understood by the people who are important to it. That means customers want to buy, donors want to donate, shareholders want to invest – and competitors walk in fear. Take a food company with a big food contamination scare as an example. People are worried – customers need to be re-assured through a consumer PR programme; corporate reputation is at stake – that means positive corporate PR; the financial media and analysts need to understand the financial impact; food is a regulated industry so the politicians will be on your back; and nervous shareholders will be asking themselves whether they should stay invested unless you have a strong IR programme in place. Get it right, and the company will sail on, with a stronger reputation than it had before. Get it wrong, and you won't have a company at all.

Jonathan Clare, Chairman, Newgate Communications LLP

"PR is about storytelling, influence, reputation and relationships, and in an ever-changing media-world transitioning from print to digital, we have never had as many ways to achieve or manage it. It's not simply about achieving press coverage - self-publishing digitally and the breadth of social media are also a powerful tools in the modern landscape."

Cat Macdonald, Communications Director, Absolute Radio, @catmacdonald

"There was a time when the term "PR" described a role that was focused pretty exclusively on press and media and was heavily reliant on 'news' release distribution supported by a few longstanding relationships with journalists. Today most people with PR in their titles are involved in a raft of communications tasks and strategies and are as likely to be developing messages to change the behaviour of customers, influence government policy and build strong internal cultures as they are providing context to specialist commentators in different types of media outlets. It is far more broad-based and much more exciting as a result."
Stewart Prosser, Director, Prosser Associates

"PR is all about reputation and creating a favourable environment to enhance the reputation of brands. However, personally I think the term PR is dead. It's all about communications. Communications is a far broader, all-encompassing term that I feel is more representative of the work that we do."
Lucie Harper, Executive Vice President, Weber Shandwick London

"What is PR is an incredibly good question. The term can sometimes be quite narrow in its interpretation, but the digital and social revolution has changed the rules completely, breaking down barriers between communications disciplines. Today's communicators need to be able to understand and advise on how organisations engage with their different audiences using whatever channel is best to make an impactful connection, rather than where "PR" is traditionally supposed to play. An understanding of the digital and social landscape is critical, but at the heart of the discipline remains rigorous strategic thinking and planning, getting to the heart of an issue, working out what will motivate people to engage and selecting the best channels to reach them. Today, it's all communications."
Simon Matthews, Chief Executive, Fishburn Hedges Group

"I remember once being shown a really long and boring paragraph about 'what PR is'. Ironic, given that PR is the art of seeing the heart of a story, and telling it as simply / powerfully as possible. It's about getting a business, an organisation or an idea onto a public platform, and giving it the voice it deserves."

Jo Burkill, PR Manager, the Timewise Foundation, @joburkill

"I am still a baby in the PR industry but I've definitely learned a lot through my experiences. The best advice I can give is to find your niche in the communications industry. I believe people can communicate the most effectively and passionately if they are talking about a subject they are interested in. My keen interest in technology led me to work for a B2B technology PR agency. Persistence is very important when trying to enter the industry, take every opportunity and don't give up."

Tajah Brown, Social Media Executive, First Base Communications, @tajah_brown

Chapter 2: What do PR people do?

If someone asked you to explain what dinner ladies, fire fighters, nurses, accountants, lawyers or lorry drivers do, you'd be able to have a pretty good stab at explaining it.

If you want your parents to proudly declare, "my daughter is a PR consultant" and for the other people at the dinner table to go "ooooooOooO! My son wanted to go into PR but settled for being a vet instead", then you are going to be sorely disappointed. Not because being a PR consultant isn't as respectable a profession as a vet, but because parents understand that vets get rid of fleas on cats, sort out their dog's arthritis and put their arms up cows' private parts to assist with bringing a calf into the world, but they don't quite have the same grasp of what PR practitioners do on a day-to-day basis. As we've already discussed, public relations is such a broad term that it covers myriad disciplines and sectors, and so there are lots of different kinds of PR practitioners – and just to confuse the matter, some of them don't call themselves PR practitioners. What they do on a day-to-day basis can therefore vary wildly.

It's all very well to say they manage reputations, but what does that actually mean? How do they do that?

Let's take a consumer PR agency as an example. They will be invited by a company to go and pitch for their business. This means they have to put together a team of people who would work on that client's account if they win the business, and a presentation of some sort to go and pitch to the in-house PR person. The pitch will include their ideas for campaigns, a timeline of how they will deliver those campaigns, a budget (the client may have specified this in advance) and possibly how they plan to measure the success of the PR work they do – some people call this the return on investment. ROI is notoriously hard to measure in PR, so some practitioners say it's not measurable at all.

In order to come up with campaign ideas they will probably have a brainstorming session with all the team members inputting their ideas. The best ideas become the pitch. It is likely that during the pitching process, several agencies will present to the in-house client, so there's no guarantee that all the hard work will pay off.

With me so far?

In this example, they win the business! Hurrah! What's next?

Well, that all very much depends on what their pitch included. They might be acting as the press office for the client, so taking incoming press enquiries. They might be doing more proactive PR and doing stunts, or events. They might be writing press releases about their clients then writing to and talking to journalists and bloggers to persuade them to run their story. They might be managing a client's social media – their Twitter and their Facebook accounts. There are lots of 'mights'. Each PR agency has a slightly different way of doing things. Every company that hires a PR agency has slightly different requirements. Every in-house PR team operates in a different way. So it is virtually impossible to give you a blueprint for a PR job, but some things remain constant.

No matter which discipline or sector you work in, you will have to build relationships; with journalists, with bloggers, with the government, and with the general public. You will have to write, and write well. You will have to manage projects and deliver to deadlines, and you will have to be prepared to have great ideas, yet change them, as the news agenda changes.

"Public relations people tend to talk a lot. This can be a good thing, but listening is also crucial in order to be an effective public relations consultant who generates value for the clients you work with, or the organisations you work for in-house.

All public relations work is delivered in a context. This may include some general factors such as trends in society and some more specific issues affecting the client organisation. These more specific matters may include the level of competition in the marketplace, threats from new technology, or levels of consumer loyalty.

Learning to listen to society, to markets and to organisations can help PR practitioners achieve a more profound understanding of the communications problems that the client – whether in-house or agency – is seeking to solve.

The most successful and professional PR people are able to demonstrate this understanding of context to the clients with whom they work. It is not an end in itself, but leads to improved analysis and the resulting communication solution delivers business value.

For those entering PR employment, active listening and questioning can lead to the "talk side" of PR work making more sense to everyone."

Gareth Thompson, Senior Lecturer, London College of Communication, University of the Arts London

"The fascinating thing is that no two days are the same. One day you could be helping to understand what is being said about your company or client by all of your important stakeholders to try to put a new business venture into context; and the next writing a short speech for the CEO to deliver at a conference or internal presentation. So it is really important to build a range of skills – from clarity of thinking, to good inter-personal dealings to working to deadlines. Being flexible while sticking to priorities, too. But these things can be learned and developed as you go."

Stewart Prosser, Director, Prosser Associates

"PR people manage reputations. This involves managing relationships with a wide range of audiences. So every day we have to think carefully about which relationships are strategically important to us. We then set about developing and implementing a communications strategy designed to promote or protect that reputation. No two days are the same, and you must be able to cope with many competing demands all the time. It can take a lifetime to build a great reputation, and minutes to destroy all your hard work."

Di Burton, Managing Director, Cicada Communications, @DiCicada

"Every day brings very different challenges for PR Professionals and no day is ever the same. One moment you can be writing a CEO speech, the next dealing with the comms fall out from a product recall and then crafting an internal campaign to launch a new IT process. That is what makes PR such a varied, stimulating and demanding career path. Its diversity and changing landscape is what makes it a challenging and rewarding."

Rebecca Salt, Group Communications Director, Balfour Beatty

Chapter 3: Agency vs in-house

First of all, let's talk about what 'agency' and 'in-house' means. A PR, public affairs or communications agency works on behalf of lots of clients at once. If it's a big agency, it may have teams split by sector or discipline, or both. If it's a small boutique agency they may focus on one particular industry like fashion, for example, or food and drink.

In-house means the PR team are working at the actual company they are doing the communications for.

There are pros and cons to working on either side of the fence.

Some people feel that if you work in-house you are closer to the company or brand and can really get under the skin of what makes it tick. You are the client (if that company has a PR agency) and so you may have to manage that relationship. Some in-house PR teams can be very small, consisting of one, two or three people, and so if you join a company like that you are very likely to be thrown right in the deep end and be given quite a lot of responsibility very quickly. On the down side, that may mean it's very difficult to get promoted, the person above you will have to leave before there is a suitable position for you to be promoted into. That's not true of all in-house PR teams though, as some of them are absolutely huge.

It is probable that at some point someone will tell you that you should start your career in an agency. They can be brilliant places to learn the craft of PR as there are lots of other PR people to learn from. You also become adept at multi-tasking and managing lots of different projects at once, as you'll be working for several clients at the same time. Career progression can also be quite swift if you prove yourself. Generally you can expect to be an Account Executive for one to two years, and then be promoted to a Senior Account Executive. However, as you're the agency and not the client, you may have brilliant ideas that your client rejects, and that can be frustrating.

My view is that it really doesn't matter whether your first job is in-house or at an agency. For the first eighteen months you will be doing pretty much the same kind of work and the danger of being pigeon-holed at this stage is slight. Any experience is good experience. Up until the eighteen month mark it is pretty easy to move from one side to the other. So you could start out in an in-house role and if you decide that actually, agency might be more for you, it's likely that an agency will be willing to hire you, and vice versa. Once you get past eighteen months it gets more difficult to move from in-house to agency, although it's still pretty common to go from agency to in-house.

Job titles vary depending on which side of the fence you're working. When you're looking for job adverts for junior roles keep an eye out for the following titles – though this list is by no means exhaustive; every company uses different titles.

In-house

Junior press officer
Press assistant
PR/communications assistant
PR/communications officer
Internal communications assistant
Public affairs assistant
Public affairs officer
PR/communications co-ordinator

Agency

Junior Account Executive
Graduate Account Executive
Account Executive
Account Assistant
Account Co-ordinator

"It's common to hear people vigorously outline the benefits of either in-house or agency roles as THE answer to junior career development. Having experienced both sides of the fence, I would recommend both. The balance of the experience may vary, with agency giving breadth, and in-house depth, but both experiences will ultimately rest on the attitude of the person going into the role. How committed are you to seeking out the views of a wide range of direct and indirect colleagues? How much effort are you going to put into developing your skills beyond that your employer provides? How much, at the end of the day, do you want it?"

Alex Pearmain, Director, Digital&Social, Brands2Life, @AlexPearmain

"I started my career in agency, have spent most of my career in-house and highly suspect I will go back to the agency side at a later stage. Both bring different challenges and require different skills. However, my advice to anyone starting out in PR is to consider the agency route at the beginning of your career as it will prove a highly beneficial foundation for the rest of your career wherever you choose to play it out."

Rebecca Salt, Group Communications Director, Balfour Beatty

"To debate Agency vs In-House is to debate two sides of the same coin, and ultimately personality steers career-PRs one way or the other. An agency position often provides exposure to wider industry and by extension a knowledge of the inner-workings of a huge array of companies; an in-house position allows for longer term strategy and a deeper knowledge and understanding of one particular company or brand. There are pros and cons to both, and those who like to look "out" often prefer the scope and variety of an agency, and those who like to face "in" find the long term brand-building of in-house positions more rewarding."

Lawrence Atkinson, CEO, DDA Public Relations, @ddaPR

"To my mind the important thing is to get hands-on experience and really whether that is at an agency or within a corporate function, the attitude should be the same. Understand as much as you can about your company or your client, its business objectives and clients. Spend time reading about the industry in which it operates – what are the issues it faces and who are its competitors? Knowing all this will help to put your work into perspective and quickly give you credibility as you begin to communicate."

Stewart Prosser, Director, Prosser Associates

"I've done both agency and in-house and both offer great learning experiences and enable you to achieve things that you'll be really proud of. I think key is to choose a company (agency or in-house) that suits your personality and character. Then move between them."

Andraea Dawson-Shepherd, SVP Global Corporate Communication and Affairs, Reckitt Benckiser PLC

Chapter 4: What are PR degrees?

In the last ten years PR degrees have become much more popular and are now offered by several UK universities. As with most degrees in any subject, it will not be vocational training. You may get a brief session on writing a press release, for example, but don't expect to get much hands-on training. Instead, you will learn about the theory of communications. The best PR degrees involve an industry placement where you *will* get the chance to put the theory into practice, so if you're deciding which PR degree to go for, keep that in mind. Most PR degrees have lecturers who have actually worked in the industry and so can give real life examples which bring the subject to life, but you should also be reading widely around the industry and building contacts from your first year onwards. Don't expect a PR degree to be a ticket to a job in PR, it is only the start of the process.

If you do decide to take a PR degree, make the most of your lecturers. As with most teachers, they really want you to succeed, so students who show willing and want to go the extra mile are always a delight for them to teach. You should also keep in touch with them once you've left university. So many students leave, never to speak to their tutors again, but they should be your first port of call when you're job hunting as invariably they will be very well connected in the industry.

If you want some more hands-on training in addition to strategic theory then it is worth checking out the Chartered Institute of Public Relations (CIPR) and Public Relations Consultants Association (PRCA) courses. Both industry bodies offer student discounts and they have some very practical sessions that should complement your degree. Alternatively, you might decide that a degree isn't for you at all, in which case it is worth investigating PR apprenticeships.

"The best PR degrees provide a 'VIP' pass to the top table of the profession. Within the framework of the latest communication thinking, a PR degree will give access to guest speakers whose reputations are both large and small, and in turn, a head start on internship and career networking opportunities. Whether it is the strategic dimension and campaign planning, or the latest specialist techniques, the PR degree can deliver these, together with insights from other academic disciplines such as psychology and politics, as well as PR's own developing body of research. It is by no means the only way into the profession – and you cannot teach everything - but for someone who is sure that it is the career for them, it can be fertile territory to discover and reflect on the latest thinking, develop your confidence, and 'hit the ground running'. It has been so exciting seeing PR graduates going on to secure great PR careers, and start to challenge established thinking about how things should be done."

**Paul Simpson, Senior Lecturer, Public Relations,
University of Greenwich and Former Head of PR, BBC
Radio 1, @dutchpaul**

"A PR degree should give the student some of the toolkit to be able to hit the ground running when they start work in PR - whatever guise that job may come in. But a good PR degree is more than that; at Lincoln we seek to develop the student's ability to think critically in the context of public relations and to consider the ethical positions of the subject before they are put in a real world situation that could make or break their career. We do not train the students but we do equip them with an understanding of the industry and how to apply the theories to practice. The best degrees offer plenty of live case work through links to local industries and live projects, plus an option to take up internships partway through the course to help students make the connections. A degree will allow the new recruit to really set their sights on working at a more strategic level than just being the 'press release monkey'.

**Jane Crofts, Public Relations Programme Leader,
University of Lincoln @jane63c**

"PR Degrees equip you with both the theory and practical skills required to get a job and then build a successful career in the PR industry. The best PR degrees have a strong practical element and good links with the PR industry, so you can start building your industry contacts while still studying. Your tutors should be experts with significant industry experience, supported by visiting lecturers who can give you an insight into the day-to-day workings of the industry. Digital and social media is more important than ever, so if you choose a PR degree then make sure this part of the programme is strong."

Ben Matthews, Head of Communications at FutureGov and Former PR Lecturer, @benrmatthews

"One of the most damning things a lecturer can hear a student say is that their public relations studies didn't help them in their first job. Maybe the student will also say that they didn't learn to write press releases in the style of their new employer. Or that their lecturer told them that AVEs are useless but their clients still want them (so that means they must be OK). Let me take you back. Not so many years ago, companies would employ bright graduates into public relations jobs and no prior knowledge was assumed. There was no demand for a graduate to have done a placement and all training was carried out 'on the job' (of course, this arrangement wasn't perfect - bad and unethical practice could be replicated across an organisation). But today, many organisations expect 'oven ready graduates' - ready to perform perfectly on their first day. This leads us on to a difficult question: What is the role of a university? Is it to carry out the training that an employer doesn't have the budget or time to do? Or is to build the critical thinking and research skills and the wide-ranging but relevant knowledge that makes a graduate worthy of having a degree or Masters to their name? Some of those qualities aren't tested in entry level jobs - but as your career progresses, you may find that your university education is actually highly relevant and helps you to differentiate yourself. For instance, being able to understand the broader context of public relations decisions in the light of business, social, and technological developments is vital if you want to move into a senior role. And having the ability to interpret and understand business plans and annual reports will enable you to speak with confidence when surrounded by accountants and senior management. And if you want respect from your peers, the ability to comment with authority on PR issues will ensure their high esteem. These are the areas in which future public relations leaders need to excel, so the question that you should be asking is whether you are acquiring this knowledge during your public relations studies."

Liz Bridgen, Programme Leader, MA Public Relations, Leicester Media School, De Montfort University, Leicester. @lizbridgen

"While a degree in PR may not be strictly necessary for those who want to break into the industry, it certainly makes the process easier. The very fact that you are choosing to devote three to four years of your life to learning about PR demonstrates a clear passion for and commitment to the industry. Many PR degrees include a mandatory work placement, sometimes of up to a year, which allows students to place knowledge gained in the classroom into context. Perhaps more importantly, the skills and experience they gain will place them streets ahead of the competition after graduation. Students on a PR degree also typically have the opportunity to develop an arsenal of industry contacts during their time at university – while on placement and on campus. These contacts can be instrumental in getting that first job and will prove to be invaluable assets into the future if maintained. All in all, if you are determined to work as a PR professional, enrolling on a university degree in the subject is an excellent and logical place to start."

Hilary Stepien, Programme Coordinator, BA Public Relations, Bournemouth University, @hilree

"A PR degree is perhaps best seen as a toolkit to equip you with a range of different tools for use in a range of personal and professional situations. For example, you will acquire practical skills such as producing great content for different contexts, you gain theoretical understanding of organisations and the forces that impact on them, you will learn about the global media environment and how to manage it. But you will also develop new abilities such as critical thinking, how to identify and make the most of opportunities that arise and learn to function as an independent and reflective individual.

But you won't achieve all this simply by turning up. You will need to read, think and act. It won't be easy, but the rewards - both personally and professionally - will be worth it."

Simon Collister, Senior Lecturer, London College of Communication, University of the Arts London @simoncollister

"A PR Degree can provide a basic introduction to the wide world of Public Relations, but cannot be relied on as a direct route into the industry. As an agency which specialises in PR for a particular sector, we seek candidates who show passion for and knowledge of our market, and who have found ways to experience it first-hand already through placements, summer-jobs, work experience or internships. I place as much emphasis on the extra-curricular achievements on a candidate's CV as the degree itself."

Lawrence Atkinson, CEO, DDA Public Relations, @ddaPR

"The question then is always about the value of PR degrees. The truth is this -as with all subjects, some university courses are better than others. That is why the PRCA endorses the courses of our 14 Partner Universities -to enable students to have some idea of why universities employers respect.

But a word of caution -if you have a PR degree, your employer is going to expect you understand the basics of PR. if they discover that you can't write grammatically and put together a fluent press release, they are going to be rather disappointed in you."

Francis Ingham, Director General, PRCA, @PRCAIngham

Chapter 5: Do I need a PR degree?

The short answer is no. By all means, study PR if you feel you'd like to spend three years learning the theory of strategic communications, but don't expect it to be a ticket to a job in the industry. In fact, some employers actively discriminate against PR degrees and much prefer broader academic subjects like history, economics or English. Some PR employers are taking a more radical approach to entry-level jobs and aren't insisting on a degree at all. Several PR agencies now run apprenticeship schemes rather than graduate recruitment schemes – so you only have to be 16+ with good GCSE's and a passion for communications.

More important than a degree, whatever the subject, is being able to show a commitment to the industry and, preferably, some relevant work experience. Some PR degrees will give you the edge on the experience front as they will require a year's work placement so by the time you graduate, you've already got twelve months of relevant experience under your belt.

"I've been teaching public relations in universities for ten years, yet even I'll admit that a degree is not enough (and a PR degree is still not essential). A degree indicates something. It should indicate curiosity and an ability to learn, and this is easily assessed at interview by asking about current affairs (or sport or popular culture). Good candidates should also have gained some work experience. They will also have the right attitude and have something to show for their time outside the classroom. Have they written for online magazines? Do they have their own blog? What about their presence on social networks?"
Richard Bailey, PR Lecturer and Editor of Behind the Spin Magazine. @behindthespin

"Do you need a PR degree? No! Although there is much discussion in the industry regarding skills-based hiring and apprenticeship schemes (and there are some good ones around, for example the scheme run by the PRCA), the vast majority of agencies use degree level study as a key criteria for shortlisting, particularly when faced with a large number of applicants for jobs or internships. In my experience, PR degrees do not give an advantage to applicants. With this in mind, I would advise anyone interested in pursuing a career in PR to gain a good degree (2.1 or above) in a traditional educationally rigorous subject (arts or science) from a respected university (yes, the usual suspects but that is the reality of the job market). Some students decide to study PR after their first degree and these courses can give a good insight into the industry but again aren't essential - though they can help with intern placements and that is very useful in such a competitive environment."

Avril Lee, Director, Luther Pendragon & formerly CEO of Ketchum, @140okay

"All education is good and having a good bedrock of theoretical knowledge is helpful, but the truth is that a strong positive attitude and proven ability to get things done can be just as important in landing a job. If you have a degree, great. But if you don't, then show that you are really interested in the industry by getting some work experience, demonstrate that you are thinking about the issues that PR, in its widest sense, can help to address and research what your employer does thoroughly. All this helps."

Stewart Prosser, Director, Prosser Associates

"You don't need a PR degree; it won't teach you everything you need to arm yourself for a career in communications. But it will be a hugely useful springboard to propel you into communications at the very start of your working life."

Rebecca Salt, Group Communications Director, Balfour Beatty

Chapter 6: Skills PR employers value

The power of being nice

There are lots of skills that are required if you are to be an effective PR practitioner, but there is one thing above all that makes you employable – being a nice person.

Do not underestimate the value of being likeable. When PR employers are recruiting, their thoughts often turn to whether they could put you in front of a client or journalist and whether that person would like you.

How to be likeable is a difficult thing to define but there are some things you should avoid doing to help you achieve it. Keep in mind that there is a fine line between confidence and arrogance. Confident people get on with a job. They ask if they need clarification on a task – as they're not scared of looking stupid if needs be – but they don't need someone to hand hold them. Arrogant people do things their own way and if they get it wrong they don't take responsibility for it.

In my time I have come across graduates who can charm their way through job interviews but invariably don't keep a job for very long as they think too much of themselves and too little of others.

So, be nice. Listen to other people's opinions. Don't ride roughshod over your colleagues, give credit to others when it's due and keep in mind that success in the public relations industry is about building relationships – and no one wants a relationship with someone who isn't likeable.

Now, on to the more tangible skills you'll need as a PR.

The number one skill

Number one on the list of skills all PR employers ask for is strong writing skills. Irrespective of sector or discipline, the ability to write well and accurately is paramount to your employability. Or, to put it simply, being able to write well makes you employable.

And there is the key – writing succinct, clear, engaging copy which is free of typos, spelling mistakes and grammatical errors is what you should be aiming for. Clear, simple English. If you are stuck in the habit of writing long academic essays now is the time to do something about it.

If you've had three (or more) years of writing essays and dissertations, how do you go about changing your writing skills to be relevant to a PR career?

Write a blog. Often people start blogging but give up fairly quickly because they feel they are talking to thin air. No one comments and they wonder if it's really worth it. Let me tell you this, the vast majority of people who view blogs don't comment. The most read post on my blog gets around 200 visitors a day – and doesn't have a single comment. That doesn't mean I'm not reaching people, it just means they have nothing to add, and that's okay. Your blog should demonstrate your interest in the industry – so keep it focussed – and is a great place for you to demonstrate your writing skills to employers. It is owned by you, so should have your 'voice' and try to steer clear of sounding too academic. A good tip is to read what you've written out loud before you publish it. Does it sound like the way you speak? If not, it's too formal.

Write thank yous. It seems that sending a thank you letter (or email, or Tweet at a push) is a forgotten art. A well-written thank you can be the difference between someone remembering you or not. If someone gives you their time for any reason, be it an interview, a conversation at a networking event, some time giving you CV advice – send them a thank you.

Write a decent CV. Your CV may be the first piece of work an employer sees, so your skills as a writer need to shine. I give my tips for writing a CV later in this book.

Write good covering letters. Do not send emails saying "Here is my CV, Regards, X". I am constantly astonished by how many people do that. How are you going to persuade an employer that you really really want their job, unless you tell them why you are so great for it? Keep it short – under 500 words – and punchy. Split the letter into three sections, which job you are applying for, why you want to work there, and what have to offer.

Write a ten-point career plan. This is just for you, not to be shown to employers, but drawing up a plan of where you want to be and how you are going to get there will make you think about achieving goals. It will also help you to work out how to write a decent to-do list.

Write on other people's blogs and industry articles. A sure fire way to get noticed by potential employers is to comment on their articles. You will also have the chance to leave your own blog URL alongside your comment, which will drive traffic to the content you've written. However, make sure your comments are relevant and don't do it too often or they'll think you're stalking them.

Write media analysis. Choose a different newspaper each week and summarise the top stories. Or choose two different papers and compare how they've covered the same story. Then post a copy to your blog and start a written portfolio – on decent paper and neatly bound – that you can take to interviews. It will be good writing practice and will be relevant content – and as a bonus you'll increase your current affairs knowledge at the same time.

Write opinion pieces. Find an industry relevant publication or website (PR Week, Communicate Magazine, PR Moment, PR Examples, Gorkana, esPResso PR news… the list is endless), research a campaign they have covered then write an opinion piece on that campaign. Was it successful? What would you have done differently? You can use your blog platform to publish it, but you should also keep it in your hard copy portfolio to take to interview. It will demonstrate that you can have an opinion and original ideas, and that you are also able to articulate them.

Write good emails. When writing to friends and family, practice writing in a business-like manner. Stay away from smiley faces and LOLs. Use the correct punctuation and pay attention to capital letters. Work correspondence is not the same as writing to your mates and it can sometimes take some time to get used to not saying "cheers" and putting kisses at the end of your messages, so it's good to get into good habits before you start in your new job.

Write a presentation. Pull together a presentation that sells you as a PR practitioner. Presentations are part of PR life – you'll pitch for new business using them, you'll use them for training, you may present to clients using them – so you might as well become a PowerPoint or Prezi expert now. You don't have to use masses of text – in fact, less is more when it comes to presentations – but relevant points and impressive visuals will make a great impression. Check out Slideshare.net for some fantastic examples.

Other tangible skills

You should also be able to demonstrate an interest in current affairs and the media. I am constantly surprised by graduates who go for jobs in PR but never read a paper other than the Metro or the Evening Standard (because they're free!) Many graduates feel that because they and their friends don't read a paper regularly they're irrelevant, but that is far from the case, and if you want to journalists to write about your clients, you need to have a good understanding of the media landscape. You don't have to buy a physical copy these days – set up a subscription on your phone or tablet – but you must invest in your media knowledge and that will probably cost you a few quid. Consider it money well spent. You should also think about the broadcast news you watch and which radio programmes you listen to. I recommend starting with the Today programme – and if you're not up early enough to listen to it, download the podcasts. You can also use online websites, and I suspect that's where the vast majority of people under twenty-five get their news from these days – but don't limit yourself to *just* online news. I guarantee that at some point you will be asked about your reading habits during an interview, so it's best to have a broad range of media to talk about. Another good way of finding out what's hot in the news is to follow journalists who interest you on Twitter.

Speaking of Twitter, it is essential that you are savvy when it comes to social media. Digital PR is now part of every discipline, across all sectors and even entry-level practitioners are expected to be up-to-date with the latest in social media developments. As an absolute minimum you should have Facebook, LinkedIn and Twitter accounts – and use them regularly. And, as I've already mentioned, you should also have a blog, which you can use to showcase your brilliant writing skills. In addition, you might want to check out FourSquare, Instagram, Google+ and Pinterest. Don't write anything on any of your social media accounts that you wouldn't be happy for a future employer to read. Employers are digitally aware and will Google you, so you can fully expect for them to be reading your Twitter feed.

When I hired junior members of staff in the past, the top items on my wish list wish list were good time management and organisational skills. PR firms want someone who can deliver to deadlines, and if they can't deliver to the deadline, be able to find a creative way to solve the problem. Punctuality is also important. Nothing is more irritating than the team member who arrives at 9.02am every morning. Yes, it's only two minutes but it's not *your* two minutes, it's company time.

You must be able to work well in a team. No one operates as an individual in the PR industry. It takes teams of PR practitioners to implement campaigns and manage the company's relationships with its stakeholders. Being a good team player is a large part of that. When you are applying for a junior job, the employer is not looking for a leader, they are looking for someone who will fit in with the team and do their fair share of work.

You should also be able to take responsibility for your work, and take criticism with good grace. You will spend quite a bit of your first couple of years receiving feedback and constructive criticism so it's essential that you learn how to accept it, learn from it, and move on. Do not sulk, or argue with your line manager, neither will enhance your prospects for promotion.

Don't be precious. You may have to do things that make you think things like "I spent three years at university and now I'm picking up doughnuts for the team," but do it anyway. I recently interviewed a Head of Communications who told me she once dressed up as Paddington Bear for a client's photo shoot, because that's what it took to get the work done. I once plumbed in the office dishwasher, and carried my boss's dog from her house to the office on the tube. Pitch in, and don't say "that's not my job".

Employers also like junior members of staff who can think ahead. It is frankly exhausting to have to micro-manage someone and tell him or her every little thing they should be doing to get the job done. Your boss will be very impressed if you can anticipate what needs to be done and ask, rather than wait to be told.

Finally, a comment on academic achievements. Some PR employers still require a 2:1 or 1st degree. Some PR employers insist that the degree be from a top Russell Group university. I would personally question those criteria for recruiting graduates. There is no doubt that you need to be smart and on the ball, but by restricting the candidate pool so much, employers are in danger of stifling diversity within their organisation. However, it is still the case that academic achievements are important and so my only advice on that front, with the danger of sounding like your mother, is to work hard and do the best you can. That said, in my experience, relevant work experience trumps academic achievements 90% of the time. So don't despair if you have a 2:2, a 3rd or even no degree at all – there are still opportunities out there for you in the PR industry.

"I must have spoken about this subject with hundreds of employers over my past six years running the PRCA. Their answer is pretty uniform -they value enthusiasm for PR, intelligence, and a willingness to work hard above all else.

What they avoid is the person for whom getting into work on time, and doing a decent day's work for a decent day's pay is the default setting."

Francis Ingham, Director General, PRCA,
@PRCAIngham

"Nothing succeeds like excess. In this case, specifically, an excess of content and commitment. Well-developed social profiles, discussing and sharing, in a realistic way, relevant industry news and content, marks you out as someone who cares, has an opinion, and has real commitment."

Alex Pearmain, Director, Social&Digital, Brands2Life,
@AlexPearmain

"I always look for people who are smarter than the last recruit. That's the way to build a great ideas-driven business. When you ask someone to do 1 and 2 and they then deliver 1 and 2 and 3 and 4 and 5 and 6 – I'm really thrilled. They anticipate your next request and then think of the new stuff that hasn't even entered your own brain. That's the kind of person I am always looking for. It's all about being restlessly inquiring."

Iain Anderson, Chief Counsel, Cicero Group,
@iain_w_anderson

"The smart students that quickly find jobs are the ones that start thinking about their future employment long before they leave college or graduate. The internet has given rise to a huge variety of publishing tools and sharing platforms that anyone can use to develop an online network and profile. I'd urge you to find a media format and platform that you're comfortable with and start creating and sharing content about your future profession. That might be a Wordpress blog, images on Flickr, or video on YouTube. Secondly, start building a network. LinkedIn and Twitter are a good place to start. Social networks are democratic and enable anyone to follow conversations taking place online. That's a short step to creating content and engaging with people throughout the industry. Start with me. I'm @wadds on Twitter. We get people walking through the door at Ketchum all the time that claim to be socially and digitally savvy yet they've never blogged and they aren't on Twitter. Do yourself a favour and get ahead of the game. It'll pay dividends personally, as these skills are much in demand, and it will help you understand the challenges that brands face in engaging with audiences in the modem media environment."

Stephen Waddington, European Digital & Social Media Director, Ketchum, and President, CIPR 2014, @wadds

"At Cubitt, we used to hire on intellect, too much I now confess, but increasingly on attitude and can-do, above core achievements; typically we look for a 2:1 from an upper quartile Russell Group university, or overseas equivalent. Our team needs to look and feel academically enough like our elite tier service firm and board level clients to be credible, but then look different enough from many of our competitors, with a strong focus on creativity and the spirit of just getting it done. We have always looked for resilience, evidence of networking even at school and university, and one thing outside work that the candidate is passionate about. Our highest value clients want a lot more than digital from even their less experienced advisers, and there is nothing to beat personal polish and confidence, elusive but vital."

Simon Brocklebank-Fowler, Founder and Chairman, Cubitt Consulting

"What skills do I value? Simple – good interpersonal skills, an ability to listen first, curiosity, proven accomplishments and a desire to make a difference a step at a time. People with these characteristics will go far."

Stewart Prosser, Director, Prosser Associates

"We receive over 1000 applications every year for fifteen graduate positions across our global business. The competition for places, and sheer number of talented and passionate candidates is overwhelming. But I understand why, because no profession beats PR for giving you the combined opportunity to engage with ideas, think strategically and creatively, or implement campaigns where you can personally make a difference in the world. So, how do you get your first break? I think you first of all need to understand the competition and the way employers filter candidates. Firstly, academic achievement matters a lot, but this is now a base line criteria. Secondly, you need to have shown a real passion for PR – no employer wants to risk a place on someone still figuring out what they want to do. The best way to showcase this is by getting involved in initiatives at university and securing work experience. We pride ourselves on building a team-orientated culture where individuals can thrive, therefore we want to hire fun and collaborative people, not lone rangers. Finally, our business is all about innovation, so we are really looking for people who have done something exceptional, however small that may be. Perhaps you have launched a charity, created an amazing digital campaign, or done something entrepreneurial. So summing up, we are not looking for the finished article, but we do want smart, passionate and fun people, who have demonstrated an ability to make a difference."

Brendon Craigie, Group CEO, Hotwire Group, @brendoncraigie

"Good PR people take care of their clients or employer, helping them connect with the wider world around them with all sorts of skills and crafts: listening, analysis, planning, writing, storytelling, image making, tweeting, posting, data crunching, idea creating and, well, the list goes on.

But GREAT PR people change the world. They help make new things possible through their clients or employers through those very same skills, PLUS, they have real passion for the power of communication.

I want the great ones."

David Gallagher, Senior Partner/CEO Europe, Ketchum, @TBoneGallagher

"I've worked in the PR industry for approaching 20 years now. For the last few years, I've provided consultancy for an American University, helping its PR post grads find meaningful work experience within blue chip PR organisations here in the UK.

The most successful candidates do share a commonality not only in their personal attributes (always learning, articulate, attentive, hardworking, humble, hungry, involved and responsive) but also in their pragmatic approach to their career.

No matter how high a star, a candidate is shooting for, when it comes to applying for their next role, the smart ones make *natural progression choices*. By that I mean they look not just at where they want to end up, but at what they could already offer and applied for the role that was next to it.

The most employable candidates have already wrapped their heads around the fact they are not going to land that dream job from 0 – 60mph but that they should build towards it in incremental and often horizontal steps.

Say you had your heart set on working in digital comms in a multi-national agency. Those candidates that have already accumulated social experience somewhere, digital experience somewhere, agency experience somewhere, and consumer PR experience somewhere are the most likely to be hired above any other candidate and then do very well once in the role.

In this climate, the successful candidate is one that views their CV as a patchwork quilt of complimentary relevant experience, rather than an elevator going up.

So having an open mind about the next opportunity is essential. And once you have secured that opportunity, immediately stop worrying about your career and focus on what your boss needs to do well and get out of the door on time and what your clients need to look good and stay happy. Trust me the career will follow."

Sam Howard, PR Consultant and Founder, The Comms Crowd, @sam_howard

"What I've learned, in what are still my infancy years in the PR game, is that you must have three core skills:

1. Excellent writing and speaking

2. Amazing attention to detail

3. Exceptional time management

If you can master the three skills above then you will be a PR star, so really work on those if you wish to excel. With regard to getting a job, I found that having a blog helped me greatly. Having a blog is a good way to market yourself, show that you can actually string together a sentence, and you can showcase yourself as a thought leader in PR. Remember, before you can learn to PR your client, you must first learn to PR yourself."
Leke Apena, Account Executive, Battenhall, @LekeDoesThis

"Have an opinion. What people hate are shrinking violets or wallflowers in the office environment. This also means doing your research and catching up with all the latest news in the media, and having a opinion about it."
Toyosi Wilhelm, Account Executive, Holst Digital, @ToyosiWilhelm

"An important part of working in communications is keeping up to date with the news, especially in your chosen niche. Social media, online publications, daily newspapers and TV are all perfect tools for keeping you up to date and providing a live news feed from both the public and journalists."
Tajah Brown, Social Media Executive, First Base Communications, @tajah_brown

"Writing competitions are a great way to prove that you can actually write. There are lots of writing competitions out there, focussing on essays, poems, stories, etc. I would suggest that you spend some time each week working on a competition entry. Not only will you constantly be sharpening your writing skills, but if you win, it will be a great addition to your CV and an interesting talking point during an interview."
Palissa Osei-Owusu, PR Intern, CNN, @Pallyoo

Chapter 7: Work experience vs internships

What is the difference between work experience and an internship? Internship is a fairly modern term, at least in the UK. Twenty or so years ago when I left university, no one did internships. They didn't exist. It was something American kids did at the White House. The UK has now adopted the terminology, but there is still some uncertainty as to what an internship should actually involve.

Work experience used to be something you'd do in your half term when you were sixteen. I once did journalism work experience at the Walthamstow Gazette. I had an article published and everything – I could not have been more excited. It was two weeks of unpaid admin work, and I very quickly realised that they were very understaffed and so anyone who could string a sentence together was an asset. So I wrote an article, which they hadn't asked for, and they printed it.

Work experience these days tends to mean a week or two of going along to a company, shadowing someone doing their job and maybe being given a few tasks to do. It should give you a flavour of the company, the industry and the job, but it's not really long enough for you to really get stuck in and make an impact. Work experience, almost without exception, will be unpaid.

Internships are a bit different to that. Generally, they tend to be at least a month long, and some internships can last as long as three, six or twelve months. There is some debate over whether internships should be paid, and indeed whether companies that don't pay interns are breaking minimum wage legislation. In my opinion, interns should be paid. Unpaid internships lead to a lack of diversity in the industry, as only people with money can afford to work for nothing. That said, there are still lots and lots and lots of unpaid internships advertised in PR and public affairs. Whether you decide to apply for an unpaid internship is something only you can decide.

However, there has been a huge push in the industry over the last five years to make internships useful for the company and fair for the intern – and that includes paying them. This swing towards paid interns has been led by the industry bodies - the PRCA and CIPR - and many PR agencies and in-house teams have signed up to say they will pay at least minimum wage. This is good news, because you'll be able to pay your rent and eat something other than Super Noodles, but it will of course mean that some companies now choose not to offer internships at all as they don't want to pay.

When PR employers are looking to employ graduates, or other entry level job-seekers, they are looking for a genuine interest in and commitment to the industry. The best way to demonstrate that is to do an internship, or two, or a few. You may find you need at least six months of experience on different internships before employers will seriously consider you for a permanent role.

Once you've managed to secure an internship, you should take the opportunity to ask as many questions as possible and volunteer to help with any work that needs doing. Don't wait to be asked. If I had waited to be asked to write an article at the Walthamstow Gazette I would have waited a very long time.

Also, keep in mind that internships can be a bit boring. The team you are working with will be busy, probably very busy if they've needed an intern to help them. Sometimes they just won't have the time to explain things, or show you how things are done. Don't be disheartened and try and find something useful to do. Don't muck around on Facebook all day – unless you're doing some research for one of their clients. Network furiously, and try to speak to as many people as possible, without being a pest.

Internships can be a really brilliant way to get a feeling for the kind of PR you're suited to, and which company cultures you enjoy working in, so make the most of them.

"In the early stages of your career, having one or more chunks of work experience will give you an advantage. Ideally in a PR agency, but stints in communications, marketing, branding or events are all good. Office administrator tasks are great regardless of the industry – employers want to see you have made an effort to build your understanding, that you have worked as part of a team, and that you have worked in an office environment. It's basic stuff, but every employer wants to feel comfortable that you will fit into their business with minimal fuss and allows them to focus on their client-driven business. A series of multiple internships is positive, as it requires tenacity to secure them. However, at some stage an employer likes to see an intern transform into a permanent employee."

Steve McCool, Founder, Message Consultants.
@mccooltweet

"The difference is usually just about length; work experience is shorter and internships longer. On some internships you'll get paid too (but not all). Go for what you can. Get variety and don't be fussy – get experience wherever you can. It shows a go-getting attitude which most employers like."

Andraea Dawson-Shepherd, SVP Global Corporate
Communication and Affairs, Reckitt Beckiser PLC

"Thinking of writing your CV? Haven't got any work experience in journalism? Back away from your PC! If you are starting out, you must get significant experience of a newsroom under your belt. Knowing about the daily pattern of a news team, understanding how the process works, seeing how a story is crafted – these things are as essential as getting work experience inside a PR agency, if not more so. After all, once you begin your career, your business will be to know their business."

Jo Burkill, PR Manager, the Timewise Foundation,
@joburkill

"The debate about work experience and internships rattles on, there are good and bad of both. There are some organisations whose business model depends upon a steady stream of undergrads working (free of charge or at best for a pittance) to get a few more lines on the CV. There are places that believe work experience means 'head of tea and biscuits'. Check out what the deal is before getting carried away by the glamour of a smart looking agency - are they going to give you some real opportunities to learn and are they going to care whether you can afford to eat? If not, ask yourself if it really counts for anything, there are some agencies that appear on almost every London-based CV... a good, small, regional agency will often give a better experience than some of the big names - simply because everyone has to muck in and work together."

Jane Crofts, Public Relations Programme Leader, University of Lincoln @jane63c

"Get as much experience as you can, work experience or internships. Volunteer in your holidays, work at a local newspaper, intern at a local company with a marketing and PR department. That real first hand knowledge will be invaluable: it shows you're hungry, alert and interested. It will also help confirm one way or other if this is the industry you want to be in. Don't be proud either – employers love someone who has shown real graft and passion."

Victoria Brough, Group Communications Director, London Stock Exchange Group

"Personally, I would not worry too much about this terminology. If you are good, then the agency will do their best to keep you and will offer you a job. If they do like you but are just not in a position to offer you a job at that time, you can always suggest to extend your internship. There have been many instances where we have offered a permanent job to a good intern. It's a good route in."

Lucie Harper, Executive Vice President, Weber Shandwick London

"Employers like us are impressed by candidates who can demonstrate that they have actively looked for opportunities to pursue their passion and build their skills and knowledge. Internships are a great way to sharpen PR and communication skills. They allow the time and space for people starting their careers to get to know and understand an organisation, its purpose and its tone of voice, all of which are essential skills in the communications industry.

London is a wonderfully diverse city and at Transport for London we want to reflect the city we serve, putting our customers at the heart of everything we do. We are proud to run two eleven month bursary-funded internships every year for candidates of BAME origin. The programme has been running since 2006 and provides a great opportunity for learning in one of the busiest press offices in the country. The scheme has supported and developed a wealth of talent from all communities and backgrounds who have gone on to establish careers in both in-house and agency roles."

Vernon Everitt, Managing Director, Customer Experience, Marketing and Communications, Transport for London

"Being a bloke of a certain age… work experience was all that was around when I started out in journalism. Internships were rarely mentioned, and it was only something kids in America seemed to do. In the UK, if you were lucky, you got some much needed work experience as a teenager and could then pretty much expect to get a job. Of course, all that has changed now (sadly!) and there is tough competition for all good jobs.

So many more young people now go for a media degree, and many of those go on to do a masters at a specialist college. This means that there is an abundance of hugely well-qualified people for employers to choose from. So, if you have to work for little or no pay for three or six months, I would say it's definitely worth it. Of course there is some abuse of this system by cynical employers, who use young people as a convenient form of cheap labour, but for most, it's a great way of showing them what you can do and how you'll fit in with the rest of the workforce. In my last job, as Head of News at Save the Children, we used a number of media graduates as interns. Without exception, they were fantastic – keen, quick, and bursting with knowledge of the latest techniques in the business. All have since found jobs either with Save or other charities. They even get paid!"

Robert Cole, Head of Communications, AMAR Foundation, @mediamacaque

"When starting out in PR, the first challenge is to get in the door! Both work experience placements and internships can achieve that aim. Good candidates often get offered permanent positions once they have completed short employment contracts in an agency or PR department. At the very least working in this way will improve your CV and your employability - and may help you pin down the type of PR you would like to work in. Generally, work experience placements tend to be shorter and not paid, compared to internships, which are usually 3+ months long and are increasingly paid at apprentice or minimum wage. Obviously for many students the first need is to be paid so that may shape your decision if you are lucky enough to be offered both types of work. Having said that, if you are offered work experience, take it!! One word of warning, unpaid work experience that lasts for long periods of time is not an ethical way for an employer to work with you, and you should pursue other opportunities."

Avril Lee, Director, Luther Pendragon and formerly CEO of Ketchum, @140okay

Chapter 8: Apprenticeships and graduate schemes

There are four ways to get a permanent PR job.

1) Do an internship and be offered a job at the end of it. This is not the norm, by the way; most internships do not lead to permanent positions
2) Go straight into a junior position, typically at press assistant or junior account executive level
3) Join a PR graduate scheme
4) Join a PR apprenticeship scheme

The difference between graduate schemes and apprenticeships seems to be this: graduate schemes are only available to graduates whereas apprenticeships are open to everyone, including graduates.

Some people will say that graduate schemes are a bit less about vocational learning and more about doing the actual job than apprenticeships, but I tend to disagree.

Both ways of entering the industry will have some element of structured learning or training. When you join a company as a junior account executive, rather than on a graduate scheme or apprenticeship, you are likely to be just doing the job from day one. Some people prefer getting thrown in the deep end like that and thrive on it, but other people like to make the transition from university and a learning environment to work and a working environment in a gentler way. Graduate schemes and apprenticeships can offer that. In the larger firms, it may also mean that you do a rotation, spending a month or so in a department and then moving on to another part of the business. This will give you a fabulous opportunity to really find out what you're interested in, and what you're good at, and you may be completely surprised : I know of some grads who had their hearts set on consumer PR but after having done a rotation on a graduate scheme ended up working in B2B tech, and loving it.

Apprenticeships are a fairly recent thing in the PR industry. Some firms have introduced them as they think they are missing out on talented people who choose not to go to university for whatever reason. Some firms introduced them because they wanted a broader ranger of people with a broader range of backgrounds in their firm in order to encourage diversity. Some graduates I've spoken to are not keen on applying to apprenticeship schemes. They resent the fact that sixteen year olds can get the same position as them, even though they have five years or more of extra education under their belt. My advice to those graduates is this: get over it. You have to play the long game. Yes, you might be recruited onto an apprenticeship scheme with sixteen year olds, but what you have, which they don't, is proven critical and analytical thinking. In theory then, you should go further and get there quicker. You have much less to learn than the average sixteen year old school leaver. Don't reject a really great opportunity to join a PR firm just because they don't ask for a degree.

For those of you without degrees, apprenticeships can be a Godsend. Until recently, having a degree was a basic requirement of getting a job in PR, but that is definitely no longer the case for quite a lot of the industry. Experience trumps education every single time. If you can demonstrate that you are really interested in the industry by having relevant work experience under your belt, you've got just as much chance as any graduate of getting your foot in the door. An apprenticeship can be a really great way of gaining practical, vocational experience in the industry and you should grasp any opportunity you are given with both hands.

"PR apprenticeships are uncharted territory as yet and so time will tell. However, it does depend on how you want to start your career. My personal view is that an apprenticeship can be a good way of finding out if PR is really for you before you commit to the expense of a degree. Apprenticeships should give the practical training that a degree cannot/should not. The degree develops that critical insight and ability to research which will allow you to rise higher in the profession to the strategic arm of PR."

Jane Crofts, Public Relations Programme Leader, University of Lincoln @jane63c

"Apprenticeships and graduate schemes are great but incredibly competitive. There are very few places and a huge number of applications. If you are not successful, do not be disheartened, I would recommend you try the intern route or, try and get in via an administrative position and work your way up."

Lucie Harper, Executive Vice President, Weber Shandwick London

"Like most professions, PR has become dominated by graduates, with a degree often seen as a pre-requisite by recruiters. That leaves a large talent pool untapped and we have found apprenticeships an ideal way to provide opportunities to people with real potential who, for whatever reason, have not gone to university. There was a good deal of scepticism in the team about the value of offering an apprenticeship and the effort that would be involved in supporting them properly. But now the post is really valued with staff recognising we get a great return on the time invested. A well put together apprenticeship will offer hands-on experience supported by classroom learning leading to a formal qualification. I'm proud of the fact that we have a 100% record of our apprentices securing permanent positions."

Mark Demery, Head of External Relations, London Assembly @MarkDemery

"Both apprenticeships and graduate schemes are excellent ways of getting into the industry. A degree seems to be the minimum now, purely because of the amount of competition for media jobs, but if you can get an apprenticeship or on a graduate scheme after that, then go for it. Like me when I left college, I was convinced that I knew the business of journalism back to front. It was only a matter of time before I mounted the steps to accept my RTS and BAFTA awards! Of course, I actually knew very little, and two years of being an apprentice on a local paper writing everything from local council reports, through house fires and burglaries, to a starring role editing the children's page, really helped mould my skills. Being an apprentice or graduate trainee of course also means that you get paid – not a lot granted - but it's got to be better that nothing at all and you will learn a lot, an awful lot."

Robert Cole, Head of Communications, AMAR Foundation, @mediamacaque

"As the industry has evolved and professionalised, the graduate schemes have become the best entry point for a long and fruitful career in the business. The best schemes attract the brightest and the best from all backgrounds, reflecting the desire of most premier league agencies to build truly diverse teams. You will find alumni of the main graduate schemes at senior levels of all the large agencies and in-house functions."

Andrew Walton, Global Head of Financial Services, Strategic Comms, FTI Consulting

"Graduate schemes can provide valuable, structured development programmes, mainly in bigger agencies, which are great for new graduates. It's a mix of hands-on work, formal training courses, team rotations and of course regular feedback. Its by no means an easy ride, and the work will be intense and hard, but it will give a great start to your career. With apprenticeships, think learning from an expert in the real world, rather than the television programme, which is about sales, hustling and short termism. Apprenticeships allow you to work with leading professional on real campaigns, absorbing as much as you can throughout the process. Either way you should always be learning. That doesn't mean constant progression, promotions and the like, but our industry changes so fast, everyone should always be learning something new, or honing a skill, almost every day."

Steve McCool, Founder, Message Consultants. @mccooltweet

"Apprenticeships and graduate schemes? Both great ways into the industry – it just depends on the individual. Apprenticeships offer an alternative route for non-graduates – perfect for those that don't want to go spend years at University. They get a structured learning and development programme while they work. The PRCA runs its own recognised PR Apprenticeship programme (www.prapprenticeships.com), on which participants work towards national qualifications equivalent to a foundation degree. Also, many top PR consultancies run schemes that are open to all entrants from all educational backgrounds.

University is not a pre-requisite for a career in PR, but it is a route that works for many. Lots of agencies run their own graduate training schemes, which can help to strengthen skills and provide relevant work experience. There's also the excellent Taylor Bennett Foundation (www.taylorbennettfoundation.org) communications training and personal development programme aimed specifically at black and minority ethnic graduates, designed to strengthen skills and provide industry relevant work experience."

Matt Cartmell, Communications Director, PRCA, @mattcartmell

Chapter 9: The importance of cultural fit

Have you ever been for a job interview and then been told that you were not offered the job on the basis that you were not the right "cultural fit". What does that mean? Are they just fobbing you off?

More and more companies are looking to hire people that not only have the skills and experience to do the job, but that also have the same attitude to work and values of their company. In fact, it is very easy to teach a new recruit new skills, but almost impossible to change their beliefs and standards towards work, so if a recruiter feels that one candidate is slightly less qualified, but a better fit for the company, it is likely that they will hire them.

Every firm has been there. An excellent candidate comes to interview. They have all the right experience and skills, they have glowing references and they sail through the interviews. They get hired and three months down the line the rest of their team is suffering from low morale and there is tension among their colleagues. This is almost always a result of poor cultural fit.

It may be that the recruit is highly competitive, while the rest of the company operates in a more collegiate manner, and so he is rubbing up his colleagues the wrong way. Or that he is extremely laid back, consistently late for meetings and joking about, whereas the rest of his team are much more serious and focussed. Hiring the wrong person for the job is an expensive mistake to make, so many hiring firms take cultural fit extremely seriously.

If you don't get a job because of "poor cultural fit", then you've probably had a lucky escape. Do you really want to work somewhere that has a totally different attitude to work to you?

To stop this happening in the future, before applying for any jobs you need to think about the sorts of corporate cultures that work for you, and then do some research on what communication companies and departments work in that way.

Have a think about your own work style. How do you like to work? Are you a nine to five kind of worker, or do you prefer your hours to be more flexible? Do you like a structured environment where there is a clear hierarchy (and therefore chances of promotion) or a flatter organisation where people share the workload? Are you a jeans and t-shirt wearing person, or do you prefer a smart suit? Do you like to socialise with your colleagues, or do you keep your work and social life very separate?

Try to be honest with yourself. Lots of people feel that they should like flatter organisation structures with more flexibility and be out on the town with their colleagues every night. But that really does not suit everyone, and some people are at their best when there are stricter boundaries and tougher targets.

The next step is to have a look at company websites. Websites are a firm's way of showcasing themselves to the world. As such, they are usually a good indication of what their culture is like. Is it very formal? Does it use very informal language? If there is a team page, have a look at what the people that work there are wearing.

If you can, talk to current or past employees of the company. Ask them to be honest about the environment and what kind of people work well there.

If you have been approached by a recruitment consultant about a position, pick their brains. A good consultant will have gone to meet the company to discuss their requirements and should have asked questions about the culture there. They may have also placed people there before, and if so will be well placed to give you hints and tips on what kinds of personalities fit well. They may also know the hiring manager, so can tell you about their working style and approach to managing their team.

Also ask your consultant about the benefits on offer, as these can be a good indication of the type of organisation it is. Firms that offer duvet days, drinks on a Friday and £500 a year to spend on a hobby of your choice may have a very different culture to one that offers private healthcare, a pension and share options.

Finally, when you are in the interview, use the opportunity to ask questions about culture. Ask them how they would describe the working environment and what kind of people do very well there.

Don't forget that recruitment is a two way street. A company is looking to see whether you can do the job, and fit into their team, but you are also trying to find out if it is the right job for you, and cultural fit is an important factor in that decision too.

I also want to raise the point about diversity here. PR is predominantly a white, middle class profession. The PR Week/PRCA Census bears this fact out, and the industry is becoming more aware that the lack of access to the profession for black and minority ethnic young people is an issue. This does not mean that if you are black or minority ethnic you will not fit into the culture of the profession. My experience of training BAME graduates on the Taylor Bennett Foundation programmes has shown me that capable BAME grads are able to break into the industry and succeed.

"I think diversity in all forms make good business sense. It goes without saying therefore, that having a workforce which is culturally diverse enables an organisation to have access to a much wider demographic of the population. Recognising that culture plays a role in how people communicate and behave, the organisation which has a culturally diverse workforce will have the edge in terms of how it communicates and adapt to different audiences. Recent findings by the IPA (Institute of Practitioners in Advertising) show Britain's Black and minority ethnic (BAME) population is worth £300 billion and accounts for 12% of the UK population. Unfortunately the make up of Britain's Public Relations practitioners still have a long way to go before it accurately reflect the ethnic make up of the country."

Evadney Campbell MBE, MD, Shiloh PR, @shilohpr

"For agencies, there are two aspects to cultural fit and we look for potential candidates who could be a cultural fit for specific clients, as well as fitting easily into our team. It is important to cultivate a "family" atmosphere within the company, whilst simultaneously being able to field different personality types to suit the particular styles of our various clients. PR agencies are only as good as the staff who work within them, so cultural fit becomes a deciding factor in any hire we make."

Lawrence Atkinson, CEO, DDA Public Relations, @ddaPR

"This is very important and people often underestimate the extent to which communications teams, especially, need to work collaboratively with others in their organisations on multiple tasks in sometimes stressful situations. Feeling you are genuinely aligned with your colleagues is essential in having a happy and successful time. The best employers are able to talk about their culture clearly and take time to ensure that new members of the team integrate happily and quickly."

Stewart Prosser, Director, Prosser Associates

"I can probably find at least five to ten good people who have the technical skills and experience for most of the roles I hire for. But finding the person with the right character, values and cultural fit is far more challenging and the area I deliberate most carefully about. I want a new person to love working in my team and I want my team to feel as though the new hire "gets it" and "gets us". The wrong decision can be awful for all concerned so the onus is one both me and the candidate to ensure we have a great mutual fit".

Nina Arnott, Head of Public Relations, Post Office, @NMEArnott

"When you embark upon a job search and begin to research the kinds of companies you're interested in working for, you'll quickly get an idea of their approach, style, priorities and any extra-curricular activity they're engaged in. Think about cultural fit while you're researching online and in meetings with recruitment professionals, and don't be afraid to ask searching questions about the company ethos and culture during the interview process.

Ideally these things should match your own approach and interests because you're more likely to get on with your future colleagues and have natural empathy for the business and culture. PR is a fast paced and often high pressured environment and feeling comfortable in the company you work for will make your life easier by removing communications barriers."

Elizabeth Adams, Director, Brunswick Group, @orangebannister

"Most firms, within and outside the industry, have a culture that is a little bit different from the others. That's neither good nor bad. It's often hard to judge before you join – but do your homework, and research potential employers. Ask during interviews about the firm's culture, practices, habits, approach to work, spirit and ethos. Then decide whether that sounds appealing to you. Not every agency suits every candidate. You may be able to get through an internship in a culture that doesn't suit you, but its not likely to be positive for either side in the longer term. Cultures change too, and you should influence the culture wherever you work. So make sure that the fit still works one year, or five years down the line. Sometimes the agency won't have the changed the way it needs to... sometimes you won't have changed to work within the agency. So a bigger change many be the best for all concerned."

Steve McCool, Founder, Message Consultants. @mccooltweet

"Finding the right organisation with the right cultural fit for you is very important to your career development and overall job satisfaction. Before taking that new job, do some cultural fact-finding. Do you agree with the organisation's values and mission? How much do you know about the leadership? Do you respect the management? What can you learn from them? Don't forget to ask lots of questions during the interview process, and really listen to the responses. Pay particular attention to what's being said and what's *not* being said. What do you *feel* when you walk into the organisation? What do you observe? How are people behaving? Ask yourself, "Can I see myself working here?" Lastly, trust your gut. Do you smell a rat? If you do, there's probably one close by!"

Gene Cleckley, Lead Manager APAC Employee and SEA Communications, ebay Asia Pacific

"It's very easy to talk about cultural fit – but what does it mean in reality? I suggest you ask yourself – are the values of the company aligned with my own personal value set. Are you interested in the projects/ accounts you will be working on and could you commit to working in that industry/ company for 2 or more years. That is a good starting part to understand culture – after all working 12 hours a day is hard at the best of times and nearly impossible if you don't enjoy or believe in what you are promoting."

Rebecca Salt, Group Communications Director, Balfour Beatty

"Picking a place to work that suits you is a very important decision. You'll probably end up spending more time at work with your colleagues than you will with your friends, families and loved ones. I know that's not an inspiring prospect but, regrettably, it's the nature of working life these days. So, if you're going to be spending a large proportion of your time working, eating, drinking and socialising with your work colleagues, the importance of a cultural fit is critical.

There's no scientific solution here, it's up to you – in your research and in your interviews – to assess the suitability of the company you are applying to. Be honest with yourself: what are the attributes and characteristics in people and organisations that you relate to and that you most admire? Are those attributes reflected in people that represent the company? Don't worry if you don't nail it first time out, this is a learning process and you can always change jobs if things don't work out. However, you'll be better off if you are honest with yourself about your professional values, do your homework and make the right decision first time round."

Dominic McMullen, Global Manager, Crisis & Issues Public Relations & Public Affairs, GE Healthcare, @dommctweets

Part 2: CVs and job applications

As far as I'm concerned, the hardest part of any job-hunting process is the written application; whether that be sending in a CV with a covering letter, or filling in an application form. It is your only chance to convince the employer that they should meet you. It is much, much more difficult to do that in writing than it is over the phone or in person – which is why applying to people you have previously met tends to have a better success rate than sending an application in cold.

PR employers are so focussed on strong writing skills and attention to detail that any mistake in your application will not be looked upon kindly. They will assume that if you can't send a perfect letter or CV, you can't write a perfect press release either.

Despite most entry-level job seekers knowing that this is common sense, they still routinely send poorly written and poorly researched applications to employers. Partly this is because of job-hunting fatigue. If you send hundreds of applications and get no responses, understandably you get disheartened. But it's no excuse. If you send just thirty decent applications you have a much better chance of securing an interview than if you send hundreds of rubbish ones.

So, in the spirit of sparing PR employers from having to read more terrible applications, the next few chapters are dedicated to showing you the error of your job-hunting ways. There is absolutely no point reading on to part three until you've mastered the written application, so take note and get ready to change how you approach job-hunting forever.

Chapter 10: Making your CV more effective

Did you know that, when a recruiter receives a CV, it is likely that they will spend no more than thirty seconds looking at it before they decide if they will call you for interview? First impressions count.

You will find that different people tell you different things about what makes the ideal CV, but the one thing everyone will agree on is that you should always aim to keep it within two sides of A4. As your career progresses it may seem impossible to keep your work history sufficiently concise, but there are a few things you can do to cut the word count and still make you sound employable!

As a basic guide your CV should include...

• Name, address, email address and phone number. You may also want to include your blog URL, Twitter ID and LinkedIn URL.

There are three essential elements to any PR CV, your education, your work history and your additional information. All three sections should use the "when, where, what" rule. Where were you, when were you there and what did you do? So for example:

June 2006 – November 2007 (when)
Absolutely Fabulous PR (where)
Account Manager (what)

• Your main academic qualifications with the most recent first, so your degree subject and grade and where you studied followed by your A Level subjects and grades and how many GCSEs you got at each grade (and confirmation you got English and Maths).

• Your work history including both paid and unpaid roles – with the dates you did the work and a short description of what you did and what skills you developed and used. Again you should work backwards through time and list your most recent (or current) job first.

• If you've worked agency side, make sure you state really clearly which clients you have worked on and which additional responsibilities you had, like line management or new business pitching. If you've worked in-house, you may want to highlight particular campaigns which you managed or crises you handled.

• The additional information section should contain everything else; training courses you've attended, languages you speak, hobbies and interests, and any work you've had published. All the things that make you an interesting person. A list of extra-curricular activities and hobbies that demonstrate further skills. If you have been involved in a lot of extra-curricular organisations, be selective, pick the ones that demonstrate specific skills and which are particularly relevant for the job you are applying for.

Personal profiles

Some people love 'personal profiles' and get quite upset when I say I'm not keen on them. Whether you have one or not is your choice, but personally I think the info you put in a personal profile is more suited to a covering letter where you can make it specific to the role you're applying for. However, if you do decide you want one, keep it short and sweet. No more than one paragraph. It should give a brief summary of your experience and any outstanding achievements and it should also make it very clear what kind of role you are looking for.

Now, here's the tricky bit, you should make sure that it is relevant each and every time you send your CV off to an employer, so it can be quite time consuming to edit it constantly. Stay clear of very generic statements like "I'm honest and hardworking" – these are basic traits that all employers will expect of you, they don't need spelling out. Similarly, "I work well in a team but am equally motivated to complete tasks on my own," YAWN. If I had a pound for every time I've read that on a CV I'd be on a beach in St Lucia supping cocktails.

Spelling, punctuation and grammar

Time and time again PR employers list writing abilities as one of the most desirable skills for PR recruits at all levels. Your CV is your first opportunity to wow them with how great your writing is, so it's incredibly important that you make a good impression. Make use of your spell check, and ensure it's set to British English, not American. Use the correct punctuation and pay particular attention to where you place apostrophes as they seem to be a bugbear of many employers. Poor use of capital letters is also a common CV crime so don't put in random capitals, or fail to use them when they are needed.

Proof reading

If you've gone to all the effort of using great grammar and a decent spell check it would be a shame to ruin all that good work by failing to proof read. Sending off a CV with typos, missing phrases and poor layout says to the employer "I'll send documents like this to your client". Would you employ someone who has no attention to detail? They won't either. Proof read it at least twice and if possible ask someone else to proof read it too, as a new set of eyes may spot things that you've missed. Things like the brand names of your clients won't be picked up by spell check if they are incorrect. My favourite example of a candidate's failure to proof read was the Account Manager who listed "murder" as one of his hobbies. It turned out he meant "murder mysteries", but he'd deleted the last word and didn't proof read before he pressed send. Scary stuff.

Layout

Think about the layout. Don't fix the problem of an excessively long CV by reducing all the text to a seven point font. Don't include lots of pictures or design elements, employers generally respond better to simple text-based CVs. Keep the layout basic and very clear. A standard Word document is fine and limit yourself to bold and underlining for headings. A clear font like Arial or Times New Roman is best, so step away from the

Comic Sans. Also, avoid using tables. Many recruiters use database software which saves the details on your CV to their system and tables can mess with transporting that data over, which is annoying and means someone has to type it in manually.

File Format

When submitting your CV by email, send it as a Word file (rather than a PDF. Imagine you're a recruiter. Now imagine you receive via email fifty CVs all called "CV". How irritating and time consuming would it be to have to rename every single document to something else so that you can find them easily on your PC? Make a friend of the recruiter and make their life a bit easier by giving it a sensible title, like your name. "Joe Smith CV" makes your document stand out against the masses of badly titled Word documents.

If you are using the latest version of Word (which by default saves files in the 'docx' format) try and choose the option which lets you save your work in an earlier version of Word, because many employers still cannot open docx files.

Common mistakes

You don't need a photo on your CV. Like it or not, people make snap judgements on appearance, albeit subconsciously, and if they've decided your face doesn't fit before they've even read about your skills and experience you've already lost the battle. Similarly, you don't need to list your marital status, your race, whether you have children or not or your age. Due to anti-discrimination laws, employers can't ask for these details.

As previously discussed, keep your CV to two pages maximum. Remember, the average recruiter makes a judgement in under thirty seconds on whether you should be called in for interview so they will never read beyond two pages. Ten page CVs are dull and time consuming to read.

If you're applying for a job in, say, food and drink PR, it is useful to highlight any experience you have previously working in that sector. It is amazing how many people will apply for a job in a particular sector and fail to highlight their experience working on a really relevant brand. Recruiters are not mind readers, they need you to point out why you are such a great match for the job description.

How to explain job hopping on your CV

One of the things employers look for when recruiting a new member of staff, is how stable their work history is. If a job applicant has jumped around from job to job over the last ten years, the recruiter's first thought will be "why don't they stick at anything?" Similarly, if an applicant has a significant length of time out of employment, the recruiter may be suspicious about why.

When you're in an interview, it's often easy to explain away jumping jobs, or being out of work but you may not even get that far if you don't make the reasons clear on your CV.

The first thing you should do is label any jobs that were short term contracts, seasonal work, or temp jobs, as such on your CV. Make it really clear that the reason you left the job is because you were only employed on a contract basis.

If you were made redundant after a short period in a job, it's OK to make a note of that too. In the current economic climate redundancy doesn't have the stigma that it had a few years ago, particularly if your redundancy was part of a large section of your firm being laid off rather than just your role being made redundant.

If you've job hopped because you've got bored in the roles, that's much harder to justify and when you secure your next position you must think carefully about sticking it out for a decent length of time, even if it bores the socks off you. Similarly, repeatedly leaving roles due to a personality clash with a boss or team member can tar you with the "uncooperative" brush so it's not wise to draw attention to why you left those roles if at all possible.

There are lots of reasons why you may have a gap on your CV. The most common being taking time out to travel, raising a family, illness or bereavement. Don't leave those gaps on your CV blank – recruiters are a suspicious bunch and will think the worst – so make sure you clearly note what you were doing during those months or years. If you have suffered with an illness it is important that you make it very clear that the condition has passed, that you are fully recovered and it will not affect your ability to work. If you took time out to raise your children, or simply to take some time away from work to reassess what you want to do with your career, then it's a good idea to mention anything you have done to stay in touch with the industry. Do you still have a good network of journalists in your little black book? Do you read industry publications? Have you take any courses to update your work skills?

By making it clear that the gaps are not anything untoward, it gives you a much better chance of getting to the interview stage where you may find the interviewer is sympathetic to your situation.

How to get the recruiter's attention

You're expecting me to tell you to do something wacky and eye catching now aren't you? Well, sorry to disappoint but on a standard CV, wacky is a bit misplaced. I once received a CV printed on Winnie the Pooh paper. What does that say about that applicant? They didn't get an interview, I can tell you that much.

However, that doesn't mean to say that creativity is always a no-no. The best approach is to research the employer, or the recruitment agency if you are applying through a third party. Are they a very formal financial PR agency? If so, a standard CV with a well-written cover letter will suffice. Are they an uber-cool digital agency? Then it might be more appropriate to do something a bit more creative.

For example, recently I saw a really lovely CV put together on Pinterest. The secret to getting the recruiter's attention is showing that you've done your homework, you know what they're all about and can act appropriately.

How to distribute your CV

Very few employers will ask you to send in a hard copy of your CV these days, but if they do then make sure it is printed on good quality white paper and is in pristine condition. Documents with coffee cup rings on them do not make a great impression.

The vast majority of your job applications are likely to be via email or job boards though, so there are a few things you should watch out for. Make sure you address the email to the right person. I've received many a CV that was quite obviously sent out to someone else previously and the sender has forgotten to change the name of the person they are sending it to.

If you are applying for a specific job you've seen advertised, make sure the reference number is in the subject line of the email so the recruiter knows immediately which role you're interested in.

If you are approaching a company speculatively, make it clear when you are available, whether you are looking for freelance or permanent work, and why you particularly want to work for that firm.

Do not send a CV without a relevant covering note, even if the job advert doesn't ask for one – that screams "I'm applying for thousands of jobs and can't be bothered to write something specific for each one". Your covering letter should be short and to the point. Which job you are applying for, why you'd be great for it and why you want to work for that company.

Use of social media

It is impossible to write a good CV guide without mentioning social media. As networking platforms continue to grow in popularity, recruiters are increasingly turning to their social media contacts to fill their roles. Make sure your LinkedIn profile is up to date. If you are able to be totally open about looking for a new role then upload your CV onto a webpage and use Twitter to publicise the URL. Finally, check out

Facebook groups like PR Job Watch which regularly have new vacancies posted on them and make it clear that you are available for work.

"Let your CV do the talking no matter what sector you wish to go into, I would recommend you put time, thought and creativity into your CV. This will be the first impression you make and it should be a good one."
Toyosi Wilhelm, Account Executive, Holst Digital, @ToyosiWilhelm

"Make your CV real, clear and tailored to the job you are applying for. Keep it simple and free of mistakes and errors. You are looking to work in comms after all!"
Rebecca Salt, Group Communications Director, Balfour Beatty

"Your CV is the first demonstrable test of your PR skills – if you can't sell yourself, then why should we trust you to communicate our organisation's messages effectively? Treat your CV like any communication: consider your audience, be clear on your key messages, tailor your product and make it compelling. Each prospective employer will be different, so ensure that your CV is the right fit – and remember that the cover letter should be complementary, not feel like two random pieces dropped in the same envelope. Most importantly, get the details right. Nothing frustrates me more in recruitment than a candidate declaring their amazing communication skills within a CV littered with spelling mistakes, poor grammar and bad English. I want to see a clear, succinct, engaging communication that connects your skills with my needs. The best CVs are a pleasure to read."
Joe Jenkins, Director of Communications, Activism & Fundraising, Friends of the Earth

Chapter 11: What to put in the hobbies section of your CV

So you've mastered the CV format and written a brand spanking new one following my guidelines but you've still got that pesky bit at the bottom to write – the bit most people call "hobbies". So what do you do if you don't actually have any hobbies? Should you leave that section blank? I think that everyone has something interesting to say about their pastimes and there are various ways you can tackle it.

Firstly, don't title that section "hobbies". Give it a broader name like "additional information" which will give you a larger range of subjects to write about. Then, start including anything that makes you interesting. Interviewers use this section of your CV to find out a bit more about you as a person, so it can help to give them a rounded picture of you. This is particularly true if you don't have much work experience – if they can't ask you about your career history, then your education and personal interests are going to feature much more heavily during the interview process.

Divide your interests into sections; sports, music, literature, art, charity, cookery, travel, etc. Under each section write something about that interest.

Here are a few examples:

Sports: Play five-a-side football for the local pub team. Manage children's under 8 team for local primary school.

Societies & clubs: Member of my university Afro-Caribbean society. Member of Little Rock amateur dramatic club.

Music: Play bass guitar in prog-rock band. Particularly keen on classical music, especially Handel.

Literature: Keen reader of historical fiction. Favourite author is Alison Weir.

Charity: Volunteer for the local women's refuge. Walked 300 miles across the Namibian dessert to raise £3,000 for a children's charity.

Travel: Travelled extensively and have visited places which include Turkey, America, Hong Kong, Australia, China, France, Germany, South Africa.

Cookery: Currently taking an evening Thai cookery course.

Crafts: I have recently completed a glass blowing course.

By fleshing out the information on each section, it gives the interviewer the opportunity to ask you about your interests in more detail. Most employers are particularly keen on activities which show you work well in a team – so playing team sports or being part of a band, orchestra or choir are always good examples of this. Steer clear of using "socialising" as a hobby – it suggests you spend a lot of time in the pub!

You should also use this section to list any further accomplishments, like additional training, any work you may have published and any posts you hold outside of work. Like this:

Training: Completed the PRCA Digital PR course, July 2012. First aider qualified.

Published Work: Author of "How to get a job in PR", published December 2013

Posts held: Governor of Little Stippleton High School. Trustee of Rocking Aid charity. At University I was treasurer of the Student Union.

Finally, you should include any skills which haven't already been featured on your CV. This may include IT packages you use and languages you speak. Make sure you clarify how proficient you are in them:

IT Skills: Advanced user of Microsoft Office, Sage and SAP.

Languages: Fluent in French. Conversational Spanish.

You might be surprised at how much you can write once you get thinking about it. Of course, if you spend all your spare time in front of the telly, now might be the time to discover a passion for something you can talk about in an interview.

"Make a decision at the start of your career to keep your private life just that - private. You'll work very hard for your employer during your working hours, and that's where your relationship ends, unless you are applying for a job in the security services. The exception is where your interests coincide with a field you want to work in, for example, sport or music. Never exaggerate your interests. My friend put on his CV he was learning Mandarin (which was true but he was at the "Hello how are you" stage), and discovered that the HR person on the panel spoke Mandarin - she conducted the first few minutes in Chinese! Beware of employers who ask interview questions about what you do in your spare time - it's a possible pathway to discrimination. What matters is what you can do at work. If an employer seems too nosey, take your talents somewhere else."

Donald Steel, Director, Donald Steel Public Relations London and former Chief Spokesman, BBC.
@LondonDonald

Chapter 12: What to write in a covering letter

Once you've got a decent CV put together you may be tempted to just fire it off to employers and recruiters, but don't. A CV should never ever, ever be sent off as a job application without a suitable covering letter. Some job adverts will actually specify that your CV needs to be sent with a cover letter, but most don't and that doesn't mean you'd get away with not sending one.

Your CV is just a statement of facts – where you were, when you were there and what you did. Your covering letter is your sales tool. Why should that company call you for interview? What can you offer them? Why are you brilliant?

As most job applications are made electronically these days, by email, you may think that you don't have to bother with a formal letter written in Word, but you'd be wrong. You want to make the process of hiring you as easy as possible, so you want your application to be easy to read, and easy to save on whatever candidate database the employer or recruiter is using. The best way to do that is to send your covering letter as a Word document, AND put the body of the letter into the email too.

The Word document should be laid out as a formal business letter with the employer's name, title (if you have it), company name and company address on the left hand side. On the next line down tab across to the right and put your name, address, mobile number and email address so that the employer can get hold of you without having to open your CV if necessary. You should then put the date.

Next you should address them with "Dear" and then their first name. So if you were writing to me you'd put "Dear Sarah". You don't need to put my surname. "Dear Sarah Stimson" sounds odd. If you don't have a name you should try your hardest to get one. Call the company that is recruiting and ask whom the applications will be going to. If you are a writing a speculative letter there is absolutely no excuse for not having a name as you should never send in a speculative application to a generic email address. Always send it to a specific person and you have a much better chance of it being read. The ONLY time it is acceptable to address a letter "Dear Sir/Madam" (with no e on madam, you're not in France), is if you have called the company and asked who the applications are going to and they refuse to tell you. The chances of that are slim.

The next thing you should include is the job reference number. If you are applying for a job in response to a job advert you've seen, it will have a job reference number on it somewhere. Some recruiters are trying to fill hundreds of jobs so it makes their life a hell of a lot easier if they can see straight away which job it is you're interested in.

Then you should split your letter into three parts.

Part 1: Which job are you applying for? You've already given the job reference number but you should also state very clearly which position you are interested in. You can do this very simply by saying "I am writing to apply for the Account Executive vacancy you have advertised on Guardian Jobs." Recruiters are always keen to know which of their adverts have been effective, so telling them where you saw the ad is a big tick in a box for you.

Part 2: Why this job and company interests you. This is your opportunity to show them that you've done your research and you know a bit about them. What pieces of media coverage have you seen recently that impressed you? What awards have they won? Have you heard great things about them from other people? Now is the time to mention all those things. However, be careful not to sound to fake and gushy.

Part 3: Why they should hire you. This is your opportunity to tell them why you are right for the job. There is a very simple way to do this. Graduates laugh when I tell them this trick, but I am telling you now, it works. Read the job advert. Adverts are generally split into four sections; a bit about the company, a bit about the job, a person specification, a bit about how to apply. The bits about the job and the person specification is what you want to concentrate on. Find all the skills and experience that they require, and all the tasks that they list as part of the job, then think of examples of times you have already used those skills or done those tasks.

For example. Let's take this job advert:

"We are an award-winning boutique consultancy that specialises in public relations and content creation for the food and drink sector. Since our launch in the UK in 2010 we have built an excellent reputation for delivering results, working for more than 1,000 different companies.

We are passionate about developing campaigns that deliver clear returns. We are great at building relationships with the relevant media for different audiences across trade, consumer and digital.

We provide strategic communications advice and campaign implementation and can offer press office and crisis management support.

We currently have a staff of thirty and are looking to grow.

Vacancy description:

You will need to be cable of carrying out research (including some work using Excel and PowerPoint) and monitoring the media to help us generate stories for our clients. You will also be involved in event management, client liaison. Supporting the teams with administrative tasks is a vital part of this role.

Person specification:

We are looking for a numerate graduate with excellent communication skills. You will need to have a good grasp of the current news agenda and a real interest in current affairs. You must be able to think creatively and have excellent organisational, communication and interpersonal skills. A proven ability to build good relationships is a must. Experience in food and drink PR is an advantage."

Right, so we've read the ad, now what's the trick to answer it? Here it is: parrot back what they say. I know right now you are thinking "really? It's not very creative to just repeat back to them everything they've asked for." But it absolutely is, because so few people do it. The way to do is it to pick out all of the important information and then give relevant examples.

From the information about the company, this is what stands out:

- Award winning agency

- 1000 clients

When you write part two of your letter, about why this job and company interests you, you can reference the awards they've won and the fantastic clients they have. In particularly you should look up some of the media coverage they've got for those clients and pick specific examples, e.g., "I was particularly impressed with the double page spread you recently achieved for Tesco in The Grocer." This demonstrates your ability to research and make it relevant.

Then you should look at the information about the job and the person specification for the tasks you will be asked to do, and the skills they are looking for:

- Research

- Event management

- Client liaison

- Administration

- Numerate

- Graduate

- Communication and interpersonal skills

- Interest in current affairs

- Understanding of the media

- Creative thinking

- Great organisational skills

- Possibly: Experience in food and drink PR

Now, find an example for each of those points to demonstrate you have all the skills and experience they need. Examples:

"I have proven research skills. For my dissertation on "The changing media landscape and its effect on PR practitioners" I had to research the PR industry in some depth and contacted over 150 senior PRs in order to complete my work."

"I am highly organised and have strong administration skills. During my time at Great Estate Agents in the summer holidays, I was responsible for handling all of their administration tasks and managed the company's diary."

And so on and so forth until you have answered all the things they have asked for. Then, as the recruiter is reading your letter she/he mentally starts ticking off all the "must have" boxes in her head.

A note here about skills and experience you might not have. In that case – do not lie. Do not make up stuff you haven't actually got. If you get to the interview, they will catch you out straight away. Instead, express an interest in developing skills in that area, e.g.,

"Although my previous PR experience was in the technology industry, I have a passion for food and drink and am particularly keen to transfer my skills into this sector."

Once you've done all that, your letter should look a bit like this:

Their name
Their job title
Their company name
Company address

> Your name
> Your address
> Telephone number
> Email address

> Date

Dear Their First Name,

Ref number:

Which job and where was it advertised?

Why this job/company interests you. What do they do that's impressive, not what can they do for you.

Why they should hire you. What can you do for them, not what can they do for you.

I attach my CV for your consideration and look forward to hearing from you.

Kind regards,
Your first name

It should be absolutely no longer than two pages, and if you can possibly manage it, one page is much, much better. When you send your email, you should copy and paste everything from 'Dear X' down to "Kind regards" into the body of the email. The email subject line should be nice and clear, with the job reference number, job title and your name, e.g.,

Junior Account Executive, REF: JAE1234, John Smith

So now you know what a covering letter should include if you're applying to a job advert, but what should you do if you are sending a speculative application?

Firstly, make sure you are writing to the right person. The best person to write to is the one you have a personal relationship with. So if you have been following an MD of an agency on Twitter and have had several (sensible) conversations there about PR, it is always worth sending your CV directly to that person. If you don't have a personal relationship with anyone at that company, call their receptionist and ask who is in charge of the team you are interested in working for, and get their email address.

Have a look at job adverts for other companies in the same sector. Invariably, they will be asking for similar skills and experience, so use those to draw up a list of relevant examples to use in your letter.

Administration features heavily in any junior PR job, so if you are writing a speculative letter, it is always good to mention how organised you are. Go back to the chapter in this book on skills PR employers value, and think about how you can demonstrate those in a letter to an employer.

Remember, each letter must be specifically tailored to the company you are applying to. You will apply for a lot of jobs, because that's the nature of the job market at the moment and there is a lot of stiff competition, but don't use that as an excuse to send out poor applications. If you write decent covering letters your efforts will pay off.

"It is essential for any aspiring PR consultant to write a good quality covering letter (or email). You would be amazed how even the best candidates don't get the content and tone right. Your letter should be no more than 300 words (your c.v. will tell the rest of the story), contain a compelling argument for your career choice and details of relevant work experience to underline your eagerness. You need to show that you understand (and have researched) the type of consultancy you are applying to with appropriate reasons for your interest. For example, applicants to public affairs companies need to know the services they offer clients – a 'lifelong love of politics' is insufficient. Do not under any circumstances address the mail Dear Sir as it betrays the fact that you can't be bothered to look up the name of the Managing Director – who may be a woman."

Charles Lewington, Managing Director, Hanover, @c_lewington

"Two main messages are important in any letter. Firstly, what you can bring to the employer - if not direct experience because of the early stage of your career, then enthusiasm, drive, creativity or the like are all good. Secondly, what you want to learn – new skills, technical know how, campaign planning, or whatever it may be. It's a symbiotic relationship and employers want to see immediate contribution from a potential employee, as well as ambition and a desire for self-improvement. One important thing to omit from any cover letter when you have less than seven years work experience – crisis management. Typically, that's the preserve of the senior team so you will just look like you are overselling yourself."

Steve McCool, Founder, Message Consultants, @mccooltweet

"I think that it's very, very important to understand the business you are writing to and the position you are looking for if you are sending a speculative letter. Make sure in the first instance you get the correct person to address your letter to! And don't ever write 'dear sir or madam': if you haven't taken time to know what sex I am then I don't have the time to read your letter. Make sure you look at the website and also Twitter feed to get up to date information on the agency and their work so you can give your letter relevance and show a genuine interest in the company. And finally don't be too sycophantic! It never works."

Nick Ede, Creative Director, EdenCancan, @nickede

"I come in to work most mornings and find at least one, if not two or three CVs and covering letters waiting for me. The ten second rule applies before the delete button gets hit – that says as much about my ruthless in-box policy as it does about my high expectations of interested candidates. 80% of emails get deleted within ten seconds, for one reason – poor targeting. My advice to applicants would be two-fold:

Target a limited number of organisations: don't email 50 companies, focus on five organisations. Get to know them, their clients, their people, their marketing effort. Play back all of this research in a bespoke cover email to those five. Flatter them about their latest new business win; tell them what you thought of their latest blogpost; congratulate them on their award shortlisting; and most importantly tell them how your skills and experience relate to their clients and agency.

Target the right people: As MD, I'm involved in hiring the senior people in the agency. Appointment of entry-level graduates is more likely to be handled by our Account Managers and Account Directors; and they don't get as many recruitment calls as me so it's easier for candidates to make an impact. Research who the middle management are, pick up the phone to them, have a conversation and let them know you are sending your CV, and then follow up with them on the phone.

It is only candidates that show interest, hunger and passion that get a foot in the Insight front door. Effective targeting and a bespoke approach have never been more important."

John Lehal, MD, Insight Public Affairs, @JohnLehal

Chapter 13: Job application tips

Four times a year I go through dozens of graduate applications for the Taylor Bennett Foundation PR programme. Each time, I am dazzled by the research and care that has gone into filling in some of these forms. And each time I am dreadfully disappointed and frustrated with others.

Having spent years processing applications and covering letters for all sorts of PR roles, I know that some of the errors made by our graduate applicants crop up elsewhere too. So for anyone thinking of applying for a junior PR role, here are some basic tips:

1. **Don't address your application to the wrong company!** Attention to detail is important to PR. Addressing it to 'Taylor Herring' instead of 'Taylor Bennett' cost one graduate a place on our programme in the past.

2. **Be polite.** And if the company you have applied to bother to reply (and believe me, lots don't) then take any rejection on the chin and thank them for considering you. Manners cost nothing. Writing to tell them that they are WRONG and are making a HUGE mistake by not taking you on will make sure they remember you for all the wrong reasons. Remember, you might find yourself applying to the same company or person again in the future, and you're going to be rejected even quicker next time!

3. **Avoid clichés.** You're really NOT thinking outside the box if you think it's okay to write "I think outside the box."

4. **If a form asks you to list your skills then saying "I'm punctual, honest and reliable"** is both dull, and not particularly informative. Surely no one would admit to be habitually late, dishonest and unreliable?

5. If you are asked "Why does a career in PR appeal to you?" do not reply with:
   a. I hear the money's good.

b. I really wanted to be a teacher/surgeon/porn star but couldn't get the job I wanted so this is the next best thing.

c. Max Clifford is MY GOD.

d. I LOVE those Guinness adverts and want to be able to create stuff like that.

e. I really want to be a journalist and think this might be an easy way in.

6. Don't ignore the "name" box on an application form. Seriously.

7. Read any application instructions carefully. If they ask for a CV and covering letter, then send a CV and covering letter. If they ask for a completed application form, then send a completed application form. If they ask for 400 words on why you'd be a great PR, then send 400 words on why you'd be a great PR. Instructions are there for a reason, so follow them.

8. Ignore word counts at your peril. If an application form asks for 100 – 200 words on a particular subject then make sure you write a minimum of 100 words and a maximum of 200. Being able to follow such basic instructions is a good indication of whether you'll be able to follow instructions once you have the job.

9. Don't submit your application after the deadline. And if your application is rejected because it's late, don't send a begging email asking them to consider it anyway. If you want it to be considered, get it in on time. There is no excuse.

10. Remember, avoid saying "I work well in a team, but also on my own".

"Reputation is about what you do, what you say and what others say about you. What you do is the most important. A reputation for reliability will never let you down. And you only earn a reputation for reliability by what you do. Most employers judge people more by their deeds than their words. You may say you are creative, digitally savvy and like meeting people (as do most people applying for PR jobs). But what about your deeds? Have you ensured there are no spelling mistakes or typos in your covering letter, CV or social media presence? Are you on time for your interview? Are you well read about current affairs, the PR industry and the organisation you are applying to? Being 'bright and bubbly' isn't enough. Nor is having a degree or even a PR degree – the latter actually increases the pressure as employers will expect more from you. There are plenty of bright and enthusiastic graduates. There are a lot fewer who are also demonstrably hard-working, thorough and reliable. Guess which ones get the jobs."

Trevor Morris, author of PR Today, Visiting Professor Public Relations at The University of Westminster and Fellow of the PRCA

"It can be hard to stand out from the crowd in a job application, but what I always look for, alongside experience and skill, is a demonstration of enthusiasm and passion. If someone has all the experience in the world I won't employ them if I don't believe they really want the job. Be as authentic as possible and don't be scared to show some personality. PR is all about relationship building and influencing so show you have thought about the company or individual you are applying to; what do you think of what they currently do and how could you improve on it? What benefit will you deliver to their business? In short, why can't they do without you?!"

Jane Fletcher, Controller of Press and Publicity, Channel 4, @Fletch100

"A career in public relations is a vocation, not a last resort. It is pointless coming to the third term of the third year of, say, a Geography degree and saying, "I am going to work in PR because I am good with people," having never considered it before then. The days of drifting into PR have gone if, indeed, they ever existed. The industry has moved on and people are deciding PR is their career of choice a lot earlier in their education. As such, getting a job in PR is becoming a lot more competitive, so you have to make sure your CV and letter of application stands out amongst the hundreds of others a potential employer will receive. The best way to do it is to populate your CV with relevant experience. Work on the university newspaper or at the university radio station; do placements at agencies during your holidays; build up a portfolio of stuff you have done off your own bat. Experience. Experience. Experience. That is what will help you get a job in PR."

Brian Beech, Managing Director, Havas PR Edinburgh/Manchester, @brianbeech

"Please do your research. Take the time to read the company website, review the latest press releases and at least Google search the business. Try and find out something about the person interviewing you – LinkedIn is a great resource. I meet so many people who can't answer the simple question 'what do you think of our website'!"

Rebecca Salt, Group Communications Director, Balfour Beatty

"PR is a physically and mentally demanding business – as well as an immensely rewarding one. You are going to be at work for long hours, thinking hard, and maybe travelling around the country or the world at pace. So make sure the employer you choose is one where you want to go to work – and they want to see you every morning.

Achieving that harmony on both sides requires an honest appraisal of your strengths, weaknesses and the type of culture where you will work best. At the same time, ensure you make an equally honest and thorough appraisal of the culture and style of working of the organisation at which you are looking. If there is a genuine match and you feel comfortable with each other, there is a much better chance of success.

Public relations has become genuinely more diverse in the sectors in which it operates, the services it delivers and the people it employs. Youth marketing and social media are important sectors today which did not exist ten years ago, for example.

This state of change in the PR industry means that the industry offers opportunities for all types of people with different knowledge and specialisms and these exist in agencies, in corporations and in the public sector. Choosing a sector where you have specialist knowledge and enthusiasm will help you stand apart – and be a better PR practitioner in your chosen area."

Gareth Thompson, Senior Lecturer, London College of Communication, University of the Arts London

"The best way to get a job is to apply! Perfect your CV and then decide what you want. Don't make things harder by applying to things you don't want – you're just wasting your time. Target the companies or roles you can see yourself in and like the sound of. Prove your skills with examples. If writing is your strength, have some examples of work or start a blog. Draft and redraft covering letters, there's always a silly mistake. Once you've written one covering letter, you can easily write another. Don't stick to the routine of looking on job sites. Many jobs aren't advertised so send out speculative applications. Look at company press sites and press releases to find the full name and contact details of people you want to work for, and if it's not online be brave and call their office for it. Let them know about you no matter how senior they are. Be confident in yourself and positive and accept that some will say no. But don't let it stop you. Someone told me to be the "good kind of pushy". See what else you can get out of them by asking for feedback, keeping in contact or even ask to meet them for a coffee just for advice. Keep applying elsewhere and back there. Nobody cares more about your career that you do, and people will respect your persistence. You will always need to be persistent when working in PR, so job hunting is just perfecting that skill!"

Monique McKenzie, Financial PR Intern at MHP Communications, @monniiqquueee

"The first thing I would advise is to really think about what kind of PR you would like to work in. I think as graduates dealing with the overwhelming stress of needing to find employment, we might just take any position which comes our way. Arguably, this could be a smart thing, because any experience is good experience. I tend to disagree with this, however, as I believe passion is really important. You will not be able to give your all and be truly enthusiastic unless you're doing something you really care about. How do you find your passion? I would advise completing short stints at different PR offices, and emailing people and asking them about their own personal experiences. Trial and error. Find ways to show that you actually want to pursue a career in PR. If you can't afford to do unpaid work experience, offer to do PR for a friend's business or arrange a virtual PR internship. Create your own opportunities. Before you make an application, I would suggest that you call up the person (if you know who this is) you will be working under and ask them some great questions about the role. Hopefully, they will remember your name when they're sifting through CV's, and through talking to them over the phone you may be able to get a sense of whether you would be a right fit for their company or work well with the person. Be determined and persistent. Every no is a step closer to a yes. I spent one whole afternoon calling all types of companies when I was sixteen years old looking for work placements as I started to think about my pension. After about fifty calls, an accounting firm said yes. You can't lose if you persevere.

Palissa, Osei-Owusu, PR Intern, CNN, @Pallyoo

Chapter 14: Using social media hunt

The world of recruitment is changing. M
recruitment agencies are turning to social media
talent. If you are looking for a job in PR how should you be
using social media tools to find your next role?

Facebook

I wouldn't recommend having an open profile on Facebook.
Most people use Facebook for keeping in touch with friends,
family and the occasional colleague and are sometimes inclined
to write things on their status updates that potential employers
would not be impressed with. I continually bore my Facebook
friends with my X Factor status updates and baby pictures –
not stuff I want to impress an employer with.

If you are going to make your profile completely open, steer
clear of status updates that say "I hate my boss", "God, work is
boooooring" or "completely hungover, cannot be arsed to go
to work so am pulling a sickie". If your profile is secure,
employers can't search for you, so that's okay.

There are other ways to use Facebook to network. There are a
couple of groups you should join; PR Job Watch and PR
Geeks. If you are not currently employed put a note up on the
wall saying what your areas of experience are and what you're
looking for. You can also have a look at the posts from
employers who are looking to hire their next PR.

Twitter

First of all, sign up! I am constantly amazed by how many PRs
are still not on Twitter. It's an amazing source of breaking news
and a brilliant way for you to network with your peers without
having to step out of your front door. Follow the right people.
If you haven't a clue who they are look at who other PR
professionals are following and use that as a guide.

You should also follow some PR recruitment agencies who will
regularly tweet about their available jobs. Then get yourself

n. Tweet regularly and retweet other people's comments en you think they may be useful. Once you are part of the R tweeting community you are much more likely to be approached by a recruiter about a new role. You could also follow the hashtags #PR and #PRjobs which will throw up a surprising amount of roles that you won't see advertised elsewhere.

LinkedIn

This seems to be the tool that most people are confused about. LinkedIn is probably the most formal of all the networking sites and as such can be really useful when looking for new jobs. Set up a profile making sure that you give details of all your past employment – it acts like an online CV and gives potential employers a chance to check out your skills and experience.

Unlike Facebook you should make your profile public, making it easier for recruiters and headhunters to find you. Then connect like crazy. Add everyone you have ever worked with, friends, family and acquaintances. The more connections you have the more likely it is that a recruiter will be able to find you.

LinkedIn's job search engine is worth a go too. When you view the results concentrate on the ones that you are no more than 'two degrees' away from – which means you know someone who knows the person who is hiring and will therefore have a better chance of being able to get in touch directly with the hiring manager.

You can also search for a specific company and see what jobs they currently have posted. You will also be able to see their recent hires so if you are feeling brave you could get in touch with them and ask how they got their jobs there – if nothing else, it might lead to a new connection.

"Aside from senior roles, which might involve a so-called headhunter, or placing ads in the PR and marketing press, social media is now the focus of most modern companies' recruitment efforts. Particularly web companies. Indeed, it's how I came to find my current role, several years ago. Not only can you find and apply directly for roles on social sites, but it's also where employers will potentially find (and judge) you. I therefore recommend spending a lot more time on your LinkedIn profile, for example, than on your CV. I've personally been put off potential candidates suggested by a recruitment agency because they don't have a LinkedIn profile, or only a very sparse one. To my mind, if you're hunting for PR work, you should be adept at managing your own reputation to begin with. Your social profile can be sent in an email or Tweeted within seconds, and it features personal recommendations in addition to your own experience and profile. It's also important to keep it up-to-date and work on building connections with people you genuinely know, even if it's college or university friends to begin with. Just as with your CV, or in an interview, never get tempted to fake it. If you're short on experience, or even if you have plenty, use your profile to bring your character, passion and skills to life for potential employers. No-one wants to trawl through mounds of dry CVs any more and seeing someone has a good sense of humour or a flair for writing can be appealing. A photograph, your connections and links to any previous companies you've worked for are just some of the other benefits of social media where recruiters are concerned - so use them to your advantage and think of it as your shop window. Finally, you can also use social media such as Facebook and Twitter to ask friends for advice and hunt around your own network for possible opportunities."

John Moorwood, Head of Communications, Wonga

"Most job applicants claim a huge enthusiasm for their chosen career and a burning desire to work for the employer they are seeking impress, so saying this in an application letter is hardly going to make you stand out from the crowd. What will boost your chances is an impressive and creative digital CV, built up over years rather than scrambled together as part of a "Help, I'm about to graduate!" panic.

Good PR is about attitude and approach, based on solid research, enthusiasm and common sense, in a fairly equal mix. These are all qualities that can shine though from a well thought out online presence. You don't have to write a brilliant blog, read by thousands every week, but you should be able to show that you are in tune with the latest trends, that you have a good visual sense, an engaging personality... as well as an attention to detail, a feel for grammar, and a working spellchecker. Make sure that if someone Googles your name - and they will - the character that emerges from your unique use of Linked In, Facebook, Instagram, Twitter and perhaps a blog, meets the job description!"

Philip Young, Lund University Campus Helsingborg, Sweden, co-author of Online Public Relations, @mediations

"The Internet is your best advantage – Create an online profile...somewhere. When creating your online profile, whether this is Facebook, Twitter or LinkedIn, remember that future employers will be looking at these profiles."

Toyosi Wilhelm, Account Executive, Holst Digital, @ToyosiWilhelm

Chapter 15: Can a quirky application secure you a job in PR?

With demand for PR jobs seemingly at an all time high, some potential candidates are employing ever more innovative methods to make their applications stand out. In a creative industry, such creative ideas in the job application process can work, though targeting is everything.

A few years ago, Lexis PR were accepting applications for their graduate scheme. Among them, one grad sent a box of cupcakes to show that they stood out... and Lexis' HR team tweeted about it, posting the above picture to the micro-blogging network.

This isn't the first time I've come across less conventional job applications. In the past I've had a graduate send me a tea bag with their CV "so that you can have a nice cuppa while you read about my experience". More recently, one of our Taylor Bennett Foundation alumni, Nahidur Rahman, wrote a blog post on why a PR firm should hire him, and Racepoint snapped him up.

Meanwhile, Graeme Anthony's CVIV (a "curriculum vitae interactive video") did the rounds on Twitter and came up trumps as he's now working at Frank. Similarly, Stephen Waddington wrote a blog post featuring Laura Tosney at 33 Digital and her (frankly, amazing) animation that clinched the job for her there – I recommend you Google it.

A few of our ex-trainees recently took part in an online chat on the Guardian website about social media careers. This led on to a discussion about how grads can make themselves stand out in the jobs market. Alan Parker of Golin suggested something quirky might work. "I once had a candidate send me a shoe in a shoebox with his CV" he told me, "so that he could get a foot in the door".

With all this in mind, on Twitter I floated the idea of a CV printed on a tea-towel (inspired by all the Royal wedding/baby merchandise). Responses ranged from "it's novel, it deserves an interview at least" from the MD of Rise PR, Paul Alan, to "that's just weird" from communications officer Emma Jackson-Stuart, and "creativity in an application isn't generally welcome in the public sector! It's better to sell yourself based on examples", from Adam Fairclough.

Which goes to show, sending a more unusual job application can work, but you have to be careful who you target with your creative approaches.

"All job applications should be tailored to the job and organisation being targeted so yes, a quirky application to a quirky organisation from a quirky person will succeed; and I have examples of quirky students who have done just that for both internships and graduate jobs. The real key is to make yourself stand out in this competitive world, PR is a creative industry so reflect that! But never try to be something you are not!"

Jane Crofts, Public Relations Programme Leader, University of Lincoln @jane63c

"Years ago our Administration Director (LB) took the trouble to read carefully a box full of CVs that had come in following a request for a graduate trainee. The person she spotted had already had a nice letter of rejection, addressed to "Dear Bobby". But as LB read "Bobby's" properly traditional CV again, she realised that Bobby was a dog. The much-loved pet of the person seeking the role. There was even a picture of him. His hobbies included "Meaterology" and positions of responsibility held "The Top of the Stairs". We were so impressed by that simple idea, so well executed, that we asked Bobby's owner in, interviewed him and then offered him a job. Nowadays he runs his own highly successful company... His CV was classic but completely different. Not gimmicky or whacky, but clever and witty. It told us more about the candidate that several A***s and a 2:1 could. I believe that he knew that if he could just get in front of someone, he stood a

chance of getting the job. There were more than 300 CVs in that box but he managed to make his stand out."
Jackie Elliot, CEO, Cathcart Consulting

Chapter 16: How to hunt for a job

1. Set yourself a specific time for job applications. If you're out of work, then treat it like a nine to five job. Get up, make a cup of coffee, turn on your computer and start hunting. Resist the urge to turn on the telly – Jezza Kyle is far too tempting. Take a break for lunch and then get back to it until the end of the working day. If you're already in a job then set aside an hour every evening.

2. Do your homework. Before you apply make sure you understand the role and the company you are applying to. Reflect your research in your covering letter and make sure each application is specific to that particular company. Standard covering letters go in the bin. If you are applying through a recruitment agency this is a little more difficult, but try to make your application as relevant to the role as possible.

3. Keep a record. A recent graduate once told me that he'd worked out it was taking him, on average, thirty three applications to achieve one interview for a PR role. That's a hell of a lot of applications but it is not surprising. Competition for roles, particularly at entry level, is fierce. I generally advise graduates to aim for twenty five applications per week, and those people who are already in jobs to aim for one application a day. With that amount of correspondence you need to keep a record of who you have written to, which position you were applying for, whether you had a response and any other info that might be useful – like a copy of the job advert or role specification so you can refer to it if you're called for an interview. Admin is tedious, but it will make your life easier in the long run.

4. Be persistent. 90% of the companies you apply to won't even acknowledge receipt of your application let alone give you feedback if you're rejected. Don't take it personally. Replying to job applicants takes a huge amount of time and administration and for some firms it's really low on their list of priorities. As a rule of thumb, if you haven't heard back from a company in two weeks, you are unlikely to be called to interview. Don't give up though. It may mean you're not right for that role, but other positions may crop up that are more suitable so keep applying.

5. Apply speculatively. If you apply for a specific job you are competing against all the other people applying for that role. If you write to a company speculatively there is less chance that you will be competing against others and therefore your letter will stand out. Make it clear what you are available for – full time, part time, temporary, permanent, contract, internships etc. Ask them to keep your details on file for any suitable vacancies and if you haven't heard back from them in three months, write again.

6. Network endlessly. Use social network sites like Twitter, LinkedIn and Google+ to follow influential PRs and get yourself noticed. Go along to Tweet Ups, conferences and social events – lots of which are free to attend. Make a point of collecting business cards and connecting with the people you have met after the event.

7. Be realistic. If you've got two years of experience and are currently paid £25,000 a year, don't apply for Director level roles paying £100,000. You'll be wasting your time and that of the recruiter.

8. Dot the 'i's and cross the 't's. Attention to detail is incredibly important when applying for jobs. Make sure you address your application to the right person, and spell their name correctly. Don't just rely on spell check to pick up errors. Proof read your CV and covering letters several times before you press send, and make sure you attach the relevant documents to your email. Good writing and proof reading skills are required for most PR roles so it's essential you can prove you have mastered the basics.

9. Pass it forward. If you spot a vacancy that would be great for a job hunting friend or acquaintance send them the link to the advert. Hopefully, they will return the favour.

10. Say thank you. If you get a personal response to your application – even if it is a rejection – write and say thank you.

If you get an interview – even if you don't get the job – write and say thank you. If someone introduces you to a contact who then offers you an interview, write and thank the referrer. Such a simple courtesy will make you stick in their minds and will make them more likely to recommend you again in the future. Thank you letters and emails are rarer than you might imagine and are a really easy way to build your reputation as a thoughtful and friendly person to work with.

"Getting a job is competitive. There are literally hundreds of applicants for every job out there.

And they're all just like you.

So you're really going to have to want that job.

You need to persuade the employers to pick you ahead of the countless others.

You're going to have to stand out.

My advice?

Treat getting a job as if it was a full time job.

Start early and work late.

Understand the industry.

Read the trade press.

Attend industry events.

Research the agency you are applying for.

Know their work.

Know their competitors.

Meet people in the industry.

Have a favourite PR campaign.

Don't take no for an answer.

Be brave.

Be awesome.

What are you waiting for?

Go make it happen.

Good luck!"
Adam Clyne, Global Commercial Director, TVC Group, @adamclyne

"Experience, Experience, Experience – These days having a degree does not differentiate you from the crowd. Show your future employers that you have taken the time to pursue your dream career, even if this means accepting unpaid work! Yes, we all have to do it at some point."
Toyosi Wilhelm, Account Executive, Holst Digital, @ToyosiWilhelm

"I began my career in music PR aged fourteen, and have been lucky to work in a variety of sectors, plus in the US. The majority of my positions have been obtained through speculative applications or networking. So my first tip for entry level seekers is INTERN, do not let working for free put you off. During this time you will make contacts and learn the basics of PR such a media monitoring, campaign planning, coverage mounting and even selling in. The PR industry is very fast paced and recruiters love people they don't have to babysit, so be proactive and ask loads of questions. If you are able to go in and carry out tasks straight away you will find you will be given more responsibility. I have found when volunteering at smaller agencies or in house teams you are given more responsibility and learn a lot more. You get a lot more opportunities like selling in to journalists, working on client accounts and assisting at events. Most small agencies or in-house teams have small staff teams and heavy workloads so they really appreciate the help - it may lead to a full time job. That is how I got my current role at the charity DiversityInCare.

My second tip would be to know what sector of PR you wish to enter. I had a lot of experience, which meant I knew the basics of PR; however, I was unsure of what direction to take, which I found made things difficult when applying for roles within sectors that I had little experience of. Remember different sectors require different skills"

Whitney Brown, Head of PR & Communication, DiversityInCare Ltd, @_whitneybrown

"My tips for breaking into PR are:

- Depending on the sector you wish to go into, ensure that you understand the most significant and relevant media for that industry. It firstly demonstrates your knowledge of the area, and also puts you ahead of other beginners as this is often something you learn as you go along
- Always research the clients of the company you are interviewing for, and use relevant examples of their work to demonstrate your understanding of the industry
- Work on time management"

Francis Graham, Account Executive, Nelson Bostock, @francis_graham

Chapter 17: Networking

I've no doubt that by now you will have asked other people what the best way is to break into the industry and I will guarantee that someone has suggested networking.

That's all very well in theory, but what actually *is* networking and how should you go about it?

In really simple terms, networking is getting to know as many relevant people as possible and building a relationship with them so that you can consider them among your network of contacts – which you may then be able to use as leverage to help launch your career.

For today's aspiring PRs there is one very obvious place to start: Twitter. Recently, I looked up all the practitioners in the PR Week Power Book 2013. A good 90% of them are on Twitter. This is a massive shift from just five years ago when social media was the preserve of junior Digital PR types. Previously unreachable senior practitioners are now available to you, the job-hunter.

To start with, I'd advise you to do a lot of listening. Follow PRs and journalists on Twitter. Follow the PR recruitment agencies and industry publications and see what other people have to say. However, you can't stay silent forever. Social media is just that, social. You have to engage with other people in order to be noticed. That is not to say you should start spamming PR agency heads in a stalker-ish fashion. You need to build a relationship with them in a soft and gentle manner. Demanding that they look at your CV is not the way to go about it.

How do you find the people to follow on Twitter? Here are a few ways to start:

PR People: this Leaderboard list:

https://www.leaderboarded.com/pr-week-power-players-of-social-media-uk-1#.Uk54UWTti3M compiled by Andrew Bruce Smith (@andismit) is a good place to start. Based on the PR Week Social Media Power Players list originally published in

February 2011, it is a comprehensive guide to those PR folk with a strong social media presence.

Journalists: Stephen Davies (@stedavies) has a great list of over 300 journalists, https://twitter.com/stedavies/uk-journalists - which is worth checking out.

Jobs: for jobs in PR there are a number of Twitter accounts worth following including @UnicornJobs, @PRJobsLondon, @vox-popPRcareers and @UKYoungPR.

Industry news: to catch up on the latest PR news follow @therealprmoment, @communicatemag, @Gorkana,@PRWeekUKNews, @Holmesreport, @esPResso_prnews and @thePR Daily.

Industry bodies: @CIPR, @PRCA_UK

And of course, you should all follow me - @gooorooo.

You shouldn't neglect the other social media platforms either. LinkedIn in particular is a natural place to start building an online network. Every time you receive an email from someone new, or meet someone for the first time, add them to your LinkedIn connections.

The idea behind online networking is that you are far more likely to spot job opportunities if you are really engaged in social media. You are also much more likely to hear directly from employers and recruiters if they know who you are, so making them aware that you are actively interested in the industry is important.

However, online networking may be a good start, but it doesn't replace face-to-face interaction. Get yourself off to some industry events. They don't have to cost a fortune. The PRCA and CIPR both run regular events which are free or cheap to attend. You should also seek out industry Tweetups and go along to those.

The thought of networking in person may make your blood run cold, but remember, PR is all about building relationships. Be brave. Very few people would tell you to sod off if you introduce yourself nicely, and ask them lots of questions. A good opening gambit is "Hello, my name is X. I've just graduated from Y university with a degree in Z and am looking to get my first job in PR. What do you do?" People *love* talking about themselves so if you can keep someone talking by asking them questions, you're doing well.

Collect business cards and follow up. Networking is less about meeting new people, and more about what you do about it afterwards. Write to the people you met and tell them how great it was to meet them. Don't ask them for anything. You should always give before you receive, so offer to do something for them; write a guest blog post, introduce them to someone else, send them an article that you think might interest them.

If you're at a networking event and suddenly find you're talking to the most boring person in the room, what should you do? There are a number of ways to extricate yourself; introduce them to someone else then swiftly leave the conversation. Pretend you have to go to the loo. Pretend you've seen someone you know and must speak to, and go and speak to someone else. Or, even if you don't smoke, say you're going outside for a cigarette.

The fact is that once you are applying for jobs, you are much more likely to be offered an interview if you have already met the person you've sent your CV to. Personal relationships make a big difference to your job prospects.

"If you don't like networking, you simply won't make it to the top of the profession, as it really is the key differentiator for mid career and senior talent. My heart sinks when colleagues tell me they are moving out of London, all too often eliminating the invaluable evening meeting opportunities which have replaced lunch for most senior people. Your income is your P&L, but your balance sheet value is in the network you build, which will be tested with acid as you move into the board of a consulting environment, or indeed in-house, where relationships which you should have invested in for fifteen years will be found out. When we launched our business we split the guest list between three co-founders, and I found I delivered 90% of the guests on the night, and guess who produced 90% of the new business for the firm over the next five years? In a business with no real franchises of the McKinsey level, hiring is most often going to be based on trust and confidence in individuals. At Cubitt, we tend to know the people who choose to work with us, based on relationships often formed outside and the business environment, so join the tennis club, a charity, or social club, and turn up and do good work, and your rewards may even be on this earth."

Simon Brocklebank-Fowler, Founder and Chairman, Cubitt Consulting

"I got my foot through the door by networking online and offline. Show your face at every opportunity, call, and email all your contacts. You'd be surprised how many people are willing to help if they see you are determined to make it. Don't be afraid to ask for help. Once you get that call for an interview that's your best opportunity to show your skills, make a good first impression and start using those very important PR skills for yourself!"

Tajah Brown, Social Media Executive, First Base Communications, @tajah_brown

"Your network is not defined by how many connections you have on LinkedIn, but by how many people would return your phone call."

Heather McGregor, Managing Director, Taylor Bennett, and author of Careers Advice for Ambitious Women

"Networking with people at the same level of the industry is key. These are the people who will form your peer group when you've all climbed the ladder, will be the people who introduce you to new roles, and as importantly, the people whose shoulders you can cry on after a tough sell-in, a bad review, or a failed pitch. These people won't just appear - but Twitte your friend. Hunt them out, and build relationships."

Alex Pearmain, Director, Digital&Social, Brands2Life, @AlexPearmain

"A talented graduate, early in his PR career, tweeted that he had lost his job. I offered my condolences and said I'd look out for anything suitable. Days later, an innovative London agency tweeted a job opportunity. I alerted him to the position; he got the job and relaunched his PR career. He hasn't looked back since. This is a fairly basic demonstration of the value of networking. But networking doesn't start with your first job or placement; it begins in your first year of university. Networking for public relations students is more than just sending a generic LinkedIn contact message to your lecturer or following them on Twitter. Most public relations lecturers have contacts with an impressive range of local, national and international employers but they aren't going to announce them to the whole class. Your lecturer needs to know the type of public relations you want to do (and where) before they can suggest people to contact. So don't see your public relations lecturer as a person whose only purpose is to help you get a good degree. They're a combination of critical friend, one (wo)man employment agency, sounding board and reference writer. But for this to happen, lecturers need to know a bit more about you. Get to know your lecturer and tell them about your aspirations and anything else that makes you stand out. Do you blog? Have you achieved any national or local recognition for your endeavours? What do you like to do? This information doesn't just allow lecturers to assist you while you are a student but also it helps them to remember you after you graduate and possibly put opportunities your way (you'd be amazed at the number of PR agencies who start their recruitment search by contacting PR lecturers)."

Liz Bridgen, Programme Leader, MA Public Relations, Leicester Media School, De Montfort University, Leicester. @lizbridgen

ǵital age, don't underestimate the importance of tworking – sharing a drink and chatting about a rest with someone can be a much richer ᴖn adding them on LinkedIn. Being able to build and maintain your personal networks – whether with journalists, stakeholders or potential clients – is a really important skill in PR, so push yourself to do it, even if you don't feel you're a networking 'natural'. I know the networks I built in the early stages of my career are invaluable to me even now, so it's well worth putting the time in to get out and meet people in person. And you might enjoy it more than you think!"

Lorna Gozzard, Head of Corporate Communications, Queen Elizabeth Olympic Park, @LornaGozzard

Chapter 18: Recruitment consultants and headhunters

Many people will meet recruitment consultants for the first time when they are applying for their first or second jobs, but might not realise the role such a person can play in helping a PR person develop a long and successful career.

A good recruiter should be a friend for the length of your career. They are also an excellent resource for industry information and gossip, particularly if you and they specialise in one area of PR, as they will have an in-depth knowledge of the movers and shakers. But what is a recruitment consultant's exact role, and what can you expect them to do for you? Here are some insights.

Firstly, if you send your CV to a recruitment agency you should be able to expect the courtesy of a reply. Even if it's to say "sorry we can't help you this time". It lets you know that your details have been received and read, and whether there is going to be any action taken by them. I am not keen on agencies which say they only respond to successful applications. It's true that it can take busy agencies quite a bit of time and effort to reply to everyone, but it is polite, and lets you know they care enough to fully consider your experience.

If the agency think that your experience is suitable for their clients they will ask to meet you. Usually this will happen very quickly as most recruitment consultancies work on a contingency basis, so they only get paid by their client if they actually hire someone they met through that recruitment agency. The job brief may have gone out to several different recruitment agencies at once so time is of the essence for that recruiter and they will want to get suitable CVs in front of their client as soon as possible. An interview with a recruitment consultant is slightly different to a job interview. They will probe you on why you want to leave your current role, and why you have left previous positions. They will also want to know what you want to do next, and why, and where you think your skills lie. Keep in mind that your consultant will be representing you to potential employers, so it is important to make a good impression.

Crucially, recruitment consultants build relationships with their client companies, which means they are the first to know when there is a new vacancy open and they get to know what kinds of people each company likes to hire – so they can advise you on the culture and requirements of each firm.

They will be able to tell you about the industry standards for salary and benefits, and give you pointers on how to improve your CV and interviewing techniques.

Your relationship with your consultant is a two way street. You should be able to rely on them to get in touch regularly to let you know of suitable vacancies, or just to catch up and see how your job search is going. You should also be confident that they won't send your CV off to any of their clients without your permission, and that they will give you frank, honest advice.

They should be able to brief you fully on any job they put you forward for and give you helpful hints and tips to get you through the interview process. If you are offered the role, they will act as your negotiator for salary and benefits, and once you've started the position, should call you to make sure you're getting on okay and enjoying your new job. If you don't get offered the role, they should give you feedback as to why, so that you can make adjustments to your approach in the future. In many cases, candidates quickly discover which recruitment consultants are working for their interests and which are just desperate to push them into unsuitable roles. The good ones really stand out, and it has been known for candidates to then become clients and use the consultant to hire their own team.

In return your consultant will need you to return their calls and reply to their emails, whether you are interested in the position they have open or not. You will also need to be clear about why you are looking for a new job, and what you want to do next. You should also keep in mind that the more flexible and open minded you are, the more vacancies they will be able to send your way. Keep in mind, though, that the vast majority of recruitment consultants work on a commission basis so that if you are placed in a job, the company who hires you pays the recruitment agency a fee. Some of the more unscrupulous recruiters will therefore push you to take jobs you may not really be interested in or suited to. If that happens, be polite but firm about saying no.

Keep a note of which recruitment agencies have sent you for which jobs so that if a consultant calls you about a position you can tell them if you've already been briefed on it by someone else. If you get called to interview by one of their clients, make sure you call the consultant afterwards to give them your feedback and to find out what they thought about you.

If you find a job elsewhere – either through another recruitment consultancy or directly – let your recruitment consultant know. Just because they couldn't help this time, doesn't mean that they won't be able to in the future and being helpful and polite ensures you are remembered. Just think, your dream job might land on their desk and you want them to call you about it.

I should mention at this point that recruitment consultancies probably won't be able to help you much until you have six to twelve months of solid PR experience on your CV. That could be a few internships that all add up to six months, it doesn't have to be in one job. Most companies find that graduates are clamouring at their doors for a PR position so don't need to pay a recruitment agency to find them. However, it's worth sending your CV off to PR recruitment agencies so that you can start building a relationship with them. Even if they don't have a job for you right now, it's worth them knowing about who you are in case the perfect position comes up in the future.

When it comes to headhunters, it is very, very unlikely that you will be approached by one at this stage in your career. Generally they work to place senior practitioners in communications roles at director level and above. If you do ever get a call from a headhunter, or meet one at a networking event, it is always worth having a conversation with them as they like to build relationships over the long-term, but don't expect them to be calling you for interview in the near future. Unlike recruitment consultancies, they don't work on a contingency basis so whether they fill the role or not they will be paid by their client providing they can show they have done all they can to find the right person for the position. Headhunting consultants are also less likely to be paid by commission, so there is less pressure on them to sell the job to you. A really good headhunter will be very well connected in the industry and will be considered an expert in their field so they are people you should aim to become friends with.

"Although a lot of organisations would probably rather not pay for recruitment consultants, if you do work for an organisation where recruitment policy and budget allows for it, they can provide an simpler service for busy teams. If you have a specific organisation or agency in mind, it's always worth a direct approach, as they'll be delighted you come without a fee. If not, look for an agency with relationships with a wide range of organisations, where you feel the recruiters really 'get' what you want to do. Personal recommendation is always a good way to find the best recruitment consultants – so speak to friends or contacts who have recently got jobs about who they recommend."

Lorna Gozzard, Head of Corporate Communications, Queen Elizabeth Olympic Park, @LornaGozzard

"I cannot understate the importance of finding a good recruitment consultant, allowing them to get to know you, and working with them to find the right position for you. The same goes of headhunters who approach you with opportunities. Remember that everyone is looking for the right fit for you the candidate, and your potential employer – the consultant's and head-hunter's client. Never settle for an opportunity you're not completely comfortable and happy with and ask them the really difficult questions you might find tricky to bring up in an interview. Double check any concerns or issues you may have discovered during your initial meetings with consultants/headhunters during the formal interview process with companies. Treat them as you'd like to be treated – be open, honest and responsive to get the best results."

Elizabeth Adams, Director, Brunswick Group, @orangebannister

"The best advice I can give is that you build good relationships with the headhunters who hunt heads in the world you work in or want to work in. These relationships could span your career, so I would encourage you to think long term and be professional. Treat meetings with headhunters as interviews; prepare, consider what impression you want the headhunter to be left with and above all be true to your self. I would listen carefully to any feedback and reflect on it. Do mine headhunters for their knowledge of the market and their perspective on your experience, skills and aspirations; working across the industry gives them a unique vantage point and they could give you the encouragement you need, or a healthy dose of realism. Consider the relationship with a headhunter as mutually beneficial; they may approach you for your dream role, give you invaluable career advice or help you broaden your network. From time to time, headhunters may ask you for recommendations; this might mean they imagine you to be well-networked with high calibre professionals in a relevant field. Do not disabuse them of this notion (!) and think carefully about who you recommend and how it might reflect on you."

Faye Wenman, Director, Taylor Bennett, @fayewenman

"The role of the recruiter can be an important one in aiding an individual in the next phase of their career and in getting that next job, not just any job, but one you actually want to be in! A lot of companies use external recruiters as they trust their professional opinions and expertise in aiding with the recruitment process, screening applications and CVs, and conducting face to face interviews to determine which candidates are best suited for said position. We all know the significance that PR plays in the reputation and the development of a company's profile and it has become increasingly important for our clients to find the brightest and best talent in the industry to be a part of that, and that's where the recruiter steps in. A lot of candidates may see us as the 'middle man' between them and their dream job, but we are very much there to put the right candidates in the right roles, to offer honest feedback and careers advice and to make sure that they are on the right path. We may not be able to get you that role straight away, but by making those initial steps and contacting a recruiter, this means you will be on their radar for when that role does come in.

Another reason to go to a recruiter is that they can open up a variety of opportunities that you may not have considered and introduce you to a wider network in the form of industry events, for example, which many of your peers, old and new, will also be invited to. I think an important factor in getting a job in PR is not to limit yourself to the opportunities out there and very much use the recruiter to answer any questions that you may have. Remember, we know what our clients are looking for!

For graduates, before you send your CV over to a recruiter, it would be beneficial for you to have at least six months work experience on your CV whether it be through internships, graduate schemes or a full time entry level position. You'll be entering a very competitive market so the more relevant experience you have, the more appealing your profile will be. Not only does it show that you're taking proactive steps to work within PR but also that you have the basic understanding and knowledge of the industry."

Seri Davies, Consultant, Unicorn Jobs, @SeriD

Chapter 19: Following up applications

If you applied for a job three weeks ago but have heard nothing will it look bad if you call them? Or should you assume you didn't get it?

The rule of thumb I would work to is if you haven't heard from a company in a fortnight it is very unlikely they want to see you for interview. It's not completely beyond the realms of possibility that they will want to meet you, but it's unlikely.

However, it's pretty useless on the part of the company or recruitment agency advertising the job. It really is mean not to get in touch at all – if only to tell you that you haven't got the job. Unfortunately, many companies are guilty of this. But it is indefensible. If they can't take you seriously as an applicant and show you some respect, why should they feel entitled to be taken seriously and treated respectfully by you? And three weeks really is a long time.

Having said all of that, you can imagine that they may have had lots of applications for the role. Particularly for an entry-level role where the average number of applications can be well over 100. If a company is expecting high numbers of applications they should clearly state on the advert that if you don't hear back by x date, you haven't been successful.

If they haven't done that, and you are still sitting there twiddling your thumbs waiting for an answer three weeks after you sent your CV, don't lose your temper. The person handling the admin may be off sick. They may have computer problems and your e-mail may have gone astray. The closing date for applications may have been extended. They may just be inefficient. So give them the benefit of the doubt and call them. Don't send an e-mail, or you risk being left hanging for another three weeks.

Check the job ad and look for a contact name and number. If there isn't one, search the internet for a switchboard number and call. Be very polite – never ever be stroppy, even if you are being treated badly – and explain: "I just wanted to check that you had received my application." If they say they have, but are still considering people, it's reasonable to ask for a rough idea of when you will know. Ask them whether they will get in touch whatever happens – and by what method: e-mail or telephone.

It certainly won't look bad if you call them – in fact the opposite. It shows you are a serious candidate who wants the job and is organised enough to chase up your application.

"There is no hard and fast rule on how best to follow-up an application. Whatever you do, make it short, sharp and memorable but do not compromise your intelligence. Show hunger, but not desperation. Maybe engage through social media."
Robert Phillips, Head of Chambers, Jericho Chambers, @citizenrobert

Part 3: Interviews

In my experience, actually getting an interview is the hard part. If you've got that far, bravo! By the time an employer has called you for interview they have a pretty good idea if you have the skills they need for the role. Your CV and covering letter should have done a good job of persuading them that you could do the tasks the role requires. The interview therefore is around 50% about probing your experience and skills and 50% about fit. Keep in mind that the interviewer really really wants you to be the right person for the job. No one wants to have to interview dozens of candidates, so they are on your side.

Cultural fit is important. The interviewer is wondering whether they would like to sit next to you for eight hours a day or whether you'd drive them bonkers. With that in mind, it's always better to be yourself than to put on airs and graces. They'll find out very quickly if you've been pretending to be someone you're not – it'll be impossible to keep up for long.

So be you, but be the best you you can be. Just as you will have to sell stories to journalists once you have a PR job, you have to sell yourself to an employer to get that job in the first place. This is your opportunity to shine, so don't waste it.

The next few chapters will give you an insight into the practical steps you can take to perform well at interview but they really boil down to just three things:

1) Be prepared
2) Be enthusiastic
3) Be yourself

Chapter 20: PR Job Interviews

Once you've cracked the application process and actually been invited to an interview, you get a chance to sell yourself. Don't waste this opportunity. Follow these ten simple rules to make sure you really shine.

1. Turn up. If you can't go to the interview for any reason, call the interviewer to apologise and explain so that they can give your slot to someone else. Not at least letting them know that you won't be there is incredibly rude and will mean you burn your bridges with that company forever.

2. Be on time. Not thirty minutes early, not five minutes late. ON TIME. If you are unsure where you are meant to be going, do a trial run a few days before. If you get there very early on the day, go to a coffee shop and hang around until it is time for the interview. If you turn up early, the interviewer will feel under pressure to interview you then, when they may have other things to do. If you are late, you are wasting their time. Being late says "my time is more important than yours". Not a great start.

3. Dress smartly. If you don't have a suit, buy one or borrow one. Polish your shoes. Have brushed hair and pay attention to your personal hygiene.

4. Take a copy of your CV, along with anything else you have been asked to take – a portfolio of work for example. You know your own CV, right? You should, but it's amazing how many people manage to contradict what they have written on their CV during an interview. Refresh your memory by reading through your CV the day before and make a note of any big achievements so that you're prepared to talk through them with the interviewer.

5. Do your research & read the papers. The company's website should be your first port of call, but don't stop there. Check our their social media channels. Do a search on PR Week to see if there are any recent industry articles on them. If you know the name of your interviewer Google them, and look them up on LinkedIn. Find out what media coverage they've received recently for their brands or clients so that you can mention it. Look up their competitors. Also, make sure you read the papers. Common questions in PR interviews include "what news stories have caught your eye recently?" and "tell me about a PR campaign you've seen in the last six months which impressed you/didn't impress you". In order to answer both of those questions you need to be fully aware of what's been in the news. Don't limit yourself to one source of news – graduates in particular are guilty of only reading The Guardian (because their lecturers do), the Metro and the Evening Standard (because they're free) and often whichever paper their parents read and is lying around at home. You need to be able to talk about a broad range of papers – both broadsheet and tabloid – and a variety of broadcast, online and radio news outlets.

6. Read the job spec or advert carefully. Make sure you are fully aware what the role entails. If the job description asks for good attention to detail, you are likely to be asked about that skill during the interview. Interviewers often use competency questions – questions which ask about past experiences to try and predict future behaviour – in order to determine if you have the right skills, temperament and cultural fit for their company. Competency questions often begin "can you give me an example of when…" or "tell me about a time that you…" For every skill or competency listed as a requirement, prepare an example of relevant experience to give the interviewer.

7. Practise your handshake. A wet fish in your hand is not nice. Likewise, don't try and crush your interviewer's hand. Firm, but not bone-breaking, is best.

8. Be interested. Don't stare out of the window when they are talking to you, or pick your nose, or stare at your shoes.

9. Be prepared to ask questions. Interviewers ALWAYS ask if you have any questions. The worst possible reply to that is "no". It demonstrates a lack of interest in the company and role and leaves the interviewer with a very poor impression of your ability to think on your feet. Before you go to the interview, make a list of five or six questions you'd like to ask about the company or position and have them written down. When the interviewer asks if you have any questions you should be able to pick at least one relevant one. If they've already covered all the things you had planned to ask you can at least point to your list and show that you had prepared appropriately.

10. Remember that an interview is a two-way process. It is your opportunity to decide if you want to work for the company, just as much as it is their opportunity to find out if they would like to hire you.

"Good PR people should be well rounded individuals with a broad range of interests including an understanding of communities and communication. You should have a passion for the media, news, social trends, visual and written storytelling. All these things will make you a creative and insightful PR professional. So... make sure you can talk about these things when you come to an interview. Demonstrate your understanding of the media (what story impressed you recently?), tell me about things that you're interested in, show me things you have written, impress me with events you have organised, and don't forget PR is a team sport, so make me see what a good team player you are."

Avril Lee, Director, Luther Pendragon and formerly CEO of Ketchum, @140okay

"It may sound trite, but to my mind, the best advice in terms of interview 'technique' is simply to be yourself. In a people business, fit and culture are vital, and there's really no point in pretending that you're anything other than who you are. Having said that, you also need to treat each interview seriously - to do your homework. Take time to work out what the questions are that you can reasonably be asked and think through your responses. For example, I've come across interviewees that proclaim on their CV that they're social media experts and yet haven't taken the time to look at my company's social media channels!"

Steffan Williams, Managing Director, Capital MSL, @steffanrhys1

"Lack of preparation is one of my bugbears in job interviews. Try and get a good amount of knowledge about the organisation you're interviewing at – look at their website, search for recent news coverage, look at their LinkedIn pages (or those of your interviewers) and other social media platforms. Try and think around their issues too – if one of their rival companies has been in the news that week, it might have had an impact on them, so make sure you know about it and have thought it through. Really communicate why you want this job, as opposed to just a job in general."

Lorna Gozzard, Head of Corporate Communications, Queen Elizabeth Olympic Park, @LornaGozzard

"I got my job through the usual interview procedure, although I think what really made me stand out as a candidate was my portfolio. Here is a little tip for youI: if you have any work that is worth showing, then show it!

I rented an iPad so that I could show some of my creative work in my portfolio. Even though this was a Junior Account Executive role, it showed that I had a creative ability, an understanding of design suites, and as well as that it showed I had the overall passion for the job *(and of course I didn't tell them the iPad was rented...).*"

Toyosi Wilhelm, Account Executive, Holst Digital, @ToyosiWilhelm

"Informational interviews are something of a myth, and underestimated by our generation, in my opinion. An informational interview is an opportunity to speak to someone who works where you want to work and/or is in a role you aspire to be in. I think this is a great way to meet people, and it shows confidence and a real drive to enter the industry. Once you work in PR you realise how important time is. If someone offers to meet up with you, respect their time by being on time, be prepared for the interview, i.e., have questions to ask, and thank them graciously. With regard to actually setting up the informational interview, if you can say you've been recommended to get in touch the person through a mutual contact, that would be great. If not, just make phone calls. At the interview stage, just be yourself, be honest, open and answer questions as fully as you can. I love preparation, and my zeal for preparation has in the past unfortunately manifested itself in a robotic and over rehearsed delivery at interviews. I'm not saying not to prepare, prepare as much as possible. Just don't come off as unauthentic. After the interview, always follow up. Someone has taken their time to interview you. Be appreciative of their time and thank them. Also, if you are not successful in your application, maintain contact with your interviewer, let them know what you're up to. The next time they're hiring, they could turn to you."

Palissa Osei-Owusu, PR Intern, CNN, @Pallyoo

Chapter 21: Job interview dress code

First impressions really count at an interview so looking your best is a must.

There are no hard and fast rules as dress codes vary from company to company, but if in doubt dress up rather than down. A dark suit is a good investment. Make sure it fits well and is cleaned and pressed. Several supermarkets now offer suits at prices to suit the budget conscious so there is no reason not to have one.

Ladies, it is no longer essential that you wear a skirt. Trousers are acceptable, but if you do choose the skirt option, keep it knee length or longer. A flash of thigh is not a good way to start an interview, nor is an eyeful of cleavage, so don't wear anything too low cut.

Shoes should be polished, shirts should be ironed, nails should be clean and hair should be washed and brushed.

Gentlemen, wear a tie. If you get to a company and realise everyone is in jeans and t-shirts then you may remove your tie, but no one will mark you down for turning up looking groomed and smart.

Keep jewellery to a minimum, and ladies, keep your make-up natural and light.

Being clean and smelling nice are essential – take a shower! But don't smother yourself in tonnes of aftershave or perfume. A small amount is fine, but if your interviewer can smell you before you enter the room it is likely to distract them.

"By the time you've done your research, you should understand the company and its business ethos sufficiently to instinctively to know how to dress for interview. If in doubt, dress smartly. Better to look overly keen than half hearted."
Nina Arnott, Head of Public Relations, Post Office, @NMEArnott

"While PR agency life is usually very relaxed, I do expect a candidate to dress for an interview as if they are meeting a client. PR is a profession, we're dealing with blue chip companies, leading brands and business critical issues so demonstrate you understand the business environment. Having said that, if you're going for a job in a sports wear company a suit and tie might not be the thing! Why not ask the HR contact or your recruitment agency what the office dress code is... aim for a level above that and you'll probably be fine!"

Avril Lee, Director, Luther Pendragon and formerly CEO of Ketchum, @140okay

"When it comes to what you wear in PR - it does matter. Even though a company's style might be quite relaxed, they need to know you can dress appropriately because external meetings may require a completely different dress code and you'll need to be able to adapt to that. I think there are two general guidelines to follow when it comes to interviews. Firstly to dress for the company you're interviewing for - by looking at the website and doing research you should be able to get a good idea of the personality of the company and that can guide you. Secondly I think it's about presentation rather than the specifics of what you wear. Better to wear a nice pair of jeans and jacket, than a smart suit or dress that is let down by a toothpaste stain or worn down shoes. Dressing the part isn't just about the company getting a good impression of you but also about you feeling comfortable – if you turn up in a suit and tie and they're all wearing shorts (or vice versa!), it will make you feel uncomfortable and less likely to interview well."

Nicola Gibb, PR Consultant, @nicgibb

"My personal approach has always been to dress smartly for job interviews, unless it's specifically stated that you don't need to. It shows that you're taking the interview seriously and also is really important for some more corporate environments. You can always dress down once you've got the job and know more about their dress code!"

Lorna Gozzard, Head of Corporate Communications, Queen Elizabeth Olympic Park, @LornaGozzard

"Dress to impress.When going for an interview, find out what the dress culture is and dress smartly, but appropriately for the role. Recruiters will be looking for someone who will fit in with their office environment."
Toyosi Wilhelm, Account Executive, Holst Digital, @ToyosiWilhelm

Chapter 22: Tricky interview questions

The thing that makes people most nervous about interviews is the thought that they will be asked a question that they just can't answer. What you should realise is that there is never a right or wrong answer to an interview question. You should always answer honestly and don't try to oversell yourself. In fact, I know of employers who are really put off by graduates who claim to be experts in PR when the reality is that the job they will be doing for the first twelve months will be heavily admin based. There are some questions that crop up time and time again, and it is possible to prepare yourself for them if you think about what the employer is looking for in your answer.

Tell me about yourself.

I am wary of interviewers who ask this question as it often means they've not spent much time reading your CV or application form. That said, they're giving you carte blanche to sell yourself really effectively. The trick with this question is to give a summary of your background, picking out the most relevant experience. Don't speak for too long – try to keep your answer to under two minutes. You can practice answering this question by having a friend time you while you speak.

Where do you see yourself in five years time?

Here, the recruiter is looking to see if you are flighty or if you are really committed to staying in this industry. Recently I interviewed some graduates for an entry level PR position. When asked this question one of the interviewees replied "Oh, I'd love to be teaching in a primary school." They didn't get the job. Declaring that your real passions lie elsewhere is not the best technique for interviews. Instead, you should make it clear that you would like to be in the industry you are interviewing for, and that hopefully you will have progressed into a more senior position. You are then reinforcing your commitment to the job and making it clear that you have ambitions to build on your skills and experience.

Why should we hire you?

How good are you at selling yourself? That's what this question really means. This is your opportunity to give a comprehensive picture of why you are better than the other ten candidates they are interviewing. You need to find a balance between confidence and arrogance. Saying "I'm the best" is arrogant. Saying "I'm the best at my current firm and have handled some really difficult and demanding clients in the last twelve months so I think I could bring some useful skills and experience to your team" is confidence. Justify your reasons with examples of your past experience.

Why are there gaps on your CV?

If you have been out of the job market at some point, it is likely it will be picked up on in interviews. The rule of thumb here? Be honest. You may have taken time out to have children, for example. Tell the interviewer that, and that you now have excellent childcare arrangements and are committed to going back to work. In the last year, many people have suffered job losses and redundancies due to poor economic conditions. Redundancy doesn't have the stigma it had ten years ago, so tell the interviewer you were one of several job losses in your firm and that although you were upset to lose your job, you realise your bosses had difficult decisions to make. If at all possible, tell the recruiter how you have kept your hand in, even when you've not been working. You may have continued to write a relevant blog, or kept abreast of your sector's media coverage. Make sure you make it very clear that you are committed to a long-term relationship with your next firm and that your break from employment was for genuinely good reasons.

What are you most proud of?

A great way to answer this is to think about an obstacle you've overcome. Something that demonstrates perseverance is always very impressive. I recently interviewed a graduate who had undertaken an Open University degree, rather than go to a campus university, so that she could be the carer for her disabled brother. That says a lot about her tenacity, and her caring nature. Who wouldn't want to work with someone like that? You don't stick to answers about university or work for this question though; have you completed a particularly difficult sporting challenge like climbing a mountain or running a marathon? Have you had work published? Have you raised significant sums of money for charity? These kinds of accomplishments all say something about you as a person, and as a potential employee.

How would your parents describe you?

I often use this question when interviewing graduates. Sometimes I change 'parents' to 'friends', 'boss' or 'colleagues'. It's a very simple interviewing technique to see if you have good self awareness and it really will make you think about how other people see you. The best way to prepare for this question is to actually ask your friends, colleagues, boss and family how they would describe you. You might be pleasantly surprised by their answers! It's also a great way of being able to say 'I'm brilliant" without sounding arrogant. If you say "I'm brilliant, you should hire me," that's a bit cocky, but if you say "my current boss says I'm brilliant. Only last week she was saying I'd done a great job at managing our latest press event and she'd be lost without me," that makes you sound very employable.

You've done a few internships now. Why didn't any of those companies hire you?

Ah, this old chestnut. In the old days if you did an internship it was quite often a precursor to hiring you. A kind of try-before-you-buy scenario. That does still happen now, to some extent, but it is much less common than it used to be. More recently, organisations have taken a more pragmatic (and ethical) approach to internships and see it as a way of offering great experience to people who are genuinely interested in the industry. They build a good relationship with you, you say great things about them and do the donkey-work that is traditionally involved in internships, and in return you get fantastic experience for your CV. They still might hire you at the end of it, but it tends to be a case of if a vacancy comes up while you're there then you're in a good position to apply for it. It's very easy to explain this situation to an interviewer; you simply tell them that a permanent position was never on the cards and you took the internships knowing that the experience was only for a short period of time, but you took them anyway because you realised it would be invaluable experience and you have a genuine interest in the industry. You can also say that by having done a few internships you now have a really good idea how different companies operate and what kind of working culture really suits you so they have been a really brilliant way of introducing you to PR.

What trends do you see in the PR industry?

Have you read the trade press? Do you read PR blogs regularly? If so, you should be able to answer this question with ease. There's no right or wrong answer, but it helps if you can quote a source, e.g., "I recently saw in PR week that revenue from CSR has increased for UK agencies over the last twelve months and I suspect that's a trend that's going to continue because...."

Talk us through your favourite PR campaign.

Here, the interviewer is testing your knowledge of a) the industry and b) what makes a good PR campaign. They may also ask you about a campaign you've seen recently which you think wasn't particularly effective. So again, reading the PR trade press is vital if you have any hope of giving an intelligent answer.

Do you have any questions?

As I suggested in chapter 20, compile a list of questions to ask – and take it with you to the interview. At the end, when the interviewer asks if you have any questions you can pull out your list and refer to it. If all your questions have been answered in the course of the interview you can say "well, as you can see I did come with a big list of questions for you, but you have answered them all already, thank you!" It demonstrates that you have done your homework.

"Time and time again, we ask candidates why they want the job. To be given supply-side thinking such as "Well, there is this gap in my CV, and working with your company will fill it." Or "I want to move closer to my boy/girl friend, and you are in the perfect place". Or "I should have been promoted by now and I don't think my [current] company really values me". Or any one of a host of responses that put the candidate centre stage instead of the company they are seeking to join. We want to know what you think you can do for our company or our clients. At this stage in the recruitment process – sorry! – I am less concerned about what we can do for you. I am really only concerned about what you can do for us."
Jackie Elliot, CEO, Cathcart Consulting

"If it is hard being the interviewee, it is even harder being the interviewer with a prospective job hunter in front of you. How do you get a real impression of someone that you don't know in just an hour? As an employer, you have spent money and time on the recruitment process and you don't want to pick the wrong person and have to go through the whole process a few months down the line. So, what you are really trying to do is ask a variety of questions. Some will just tease out a candidate's experience. However, you are always aware that someone in PR might have to think quickly on their feet, especially when faced with a persistent journalist on the telephone. Therefore, in an job interview, I am really looking to probe that ability. The usual questions won't do it, only tricky questions might. I have asked candidates what their worst quality is, what their most embarrassing moment was and how they got out of it, would they ever lie in order to stop a journalist finding out something, and would you be prepared to steal a good idea from someone else? These are all questions where answers don't come easily to mind. What I really want from them is an indication that someone has a supple and flexible mind. They are also the questions that might allow a candidate to display a sense of humour, always crucial to handling pressure in PR! So, don't worry about giving a right or wrong answer, these questions are about showing character."

Jonathan Charles, Director of Communications, European Bank for Reconstruction and Development, @ebrdcharles

Chapter 23: What weaknesses can I admit to?

The 'what are your strengths and weaknesses' question seem to throw a lot of interviewees, even though they are often expecting to be asked it. So what is the best way to answer it?

If it's any consolation, this is not a particularly clever interview question, as there is little way of gauging the accuracy of a candidate's reply. I think it's a bit lazy, but a lot of interviewers ask it. That said, you need to think carefully about your answer, because in the absence of any context, the interviewer could take your response very literally. For example, "I am not strong on the numbers side of things" may be interpreted as "he or she can't manage budgets". They are looking to see how self-critical you can be and whether you can give a balanced view. The strength side of things tends not to be too difficult, particularly if you have a job description or advert to work from. If they have asked for someone with a good eye for detail in the advert, it is a good idea to pick that out as a strength and give an example. So you could say something like "I am a stickler for detail. In my current role my colleagues always ask me to proof read their work as I am anal about typos and grammar." The weaknesses element of this question is more difficult. The most common answer I have heard is "It can take me a while to get things done, because I'm such a perfectionist." Yawn. I guarantee every recruiter has heard interviewees say that a million times. The basis of the answer is sound – pick something negative and turn it into a positive – but the answer itself is rather hackneyed. First, in your response, keep your answer very work-specific – hopefully this is common sense. Don't be tempted to take the "I am too hard on myself", general observation route.

Pick something you know you are weaker on but that you are aware of and do something about. For example, you could say "I am terribly impatient and get annoyed when other members of the team don't deliver in time, but I have learned over the years that everyone's working style is different so I try to be more laid back about it now and offer to help the others so that we meet the deadlines."

Second, think of the answer to a slightly different question: "In which areas would I like to develop additional skills and experience?" This will position your response in a more positive and proactive light. So if you feel yourself a little weak on the numbers side, you could answer, "I would love to have the additional opportunity to manage client budgets to deepen my understanding of the company's business objectives. I know that would allow me to provide increased value in my role".

"This has become a rather too common question in interviews, so most interviewees have become sufficiently self-aware to admit to some weaknesses. The stock reply is to confess to being too much of a perfectionist, or even to working too hard – so that the acknowledged weakness is really a perceived strength. My advice would be to give serious consideration to this question in advance of an interview, particularly in relation to the job in question. It's perfectly normal and human to have some concerns about the relevance of your skills and experience for any given role, and you should be given credit for sharing these with a potential employer."
Neil Hedges, Senior Partner, Headland, @NeilHedges3

"If you don't have much work experience it can be hard for an interviewer to find topics to discuss. In these situations the interviewee who says their only weakness is that they are too demanding of themselves or some such blandishment can be a little frustrating. Much better to be honest and admit to a liking for X-Factor or chocolate biscuits. It is pretty likely the interviewer will also have a view on these and it will help convince them that you are someone the team would like to work with."
Giles Fraser, Co-Founder, Brands2Life, @gilesfraser

"The "what are your weaknesses" question ranks high on my list of silly interview questions with "where do you want to be in ten years time?" Just be ready with answers to them - "I suppose my biggest weakness is that I tend to over-deliver in a job. Because I'm ruthless about meeting deadlines, I put myself under stress sometimes". A hard worker who meets deadlines - get the offer letter typed up. And where do I want to be in ten years - "I've been very focussed on getting my first job/next job. I feel the world of public relations is changing so rapidly that it's difficult to predict the direction you will take. I really want to learn and I'm convinced this company is the best place to do that." NEVER say "In ten years time I want your job". It comes across as cheeky and not in a good way."

Donald Steel, Director, Donald Steel Public Relations London, and former Chief Spokesman, BBC @LondonDonald

"Be honest – don't call them weaknesses but challenges in the role. Show you have thought it through and that you are aware of them – that's half the battle to resolving them!"

Rebecca Salt, Group Communications Director, Balfour Beatty

Chapter 24: What questions can I ask?

First of all, it's really important that you do ask a question. It shows that you've been listening, that you want the job and that you are taking the whole process seriously. It's often the last thing that they will ask you, so if you just mutter 'No', then there is the danger that the interview will fizzle out and end on a low note. And of course, you want to walk out of that room on a high, leaving them in no doubt that you are a capable, switched-on candidate.

Something may well come up during the interview that you genuinely don't understand or want to find out more about. So ask. But you must make sure that you have prepared a couple of questions in advance too. As established, it's a good idea to take along a list of around ten questions which you can whip out and refer to.

A good place to start is the company's website. Show an interest in what they do – even the parts of the business that you might have little to do with if you get the job. It will show them that you have done your homework. Other good topics include asking about training. Is there any? This shows that you want to develop within the business – and it also demonstrates a commitment to stay.

You could ask: "What kind of role could I expect to do in a year or two's time, assuming I do well in this job?" This sends a similar message. Just be careful that it doesn't sound like you're saying "how long do I have to do this boring job before I can do something more interesting?"

The main point is to be prepared. The more preparation you do for any interview, the more confident you will be and the better it will go.

By the way, some questions are taboo, such as: "What on earth made you choose that software?" "Can I wear my piercing?" "How much sick leave am I entitled to?" Avoid.

"Interviews are tricky things to negotiate. You need to understand as clearly as possible what it is that the organisation is looking for, as early as possible in the process. Most agencies want people with relevant experience which clients will appreciate and want to pay for. If you are starting out you need to find as much of it - through work experience, internships or by demonstrating your understanding of what the job might entail - as possible.

They also want to know that you'd appreciate the opportunity you are being interviewed for, will work hard to get yourself up to speed, and relish doing the basic requirements of a role quickly and efficiently to free up your time to learn from others. Especially with junior roles people are often looking for someone to come in and take a burden away from others which is something that we can sometimes forget. Whilst people want to know that you are ambitious, they will have a timescale in mind that it will take you to master the role and then a sense of how long before you will be ready to progress. It's important to look like you want this role... not the next one straight away.

When thinking about asking questions you should stick to things that you shouldn't be expected to have found out from the company's website or recent press coverage - there's nothing more telling than someone who hasn't done their research. Find some news or case studies in your research to ask some questions about. But if you are stuck - it's quite legitimate to ask what people in your role would say if you asked them what it is like to work for the company. Similarly you could ask the interviewer to describe a working week in the role. You could ask them what they think the biggest challenges in the role are too, but be prepared to talk about how you might meet them. There are subtle ways to ask about career progression - by asking what previous incumbents went on to do, for example, if you want to show you are interested in the future of the company. Finally... it's really important to ask the interviewer if they have any concerns about what you have told them... so that you can answer there and then any issues about your application because you may not get a second chance. And then... don't wait to be prompted. Tell them everything you have heard has only made you more determined to work for them!"

Nick Clark, Managing Director, Consolidated PR, @prboy

"Two basic rules: make sure you arrive at an interview with some questions to ask and make sure the answers to these questions aren't on the homepage of the company's website. If someone is considering employing you, one of the things they'll want evidence of is a genuine interest in their company, but they'll also want to know that you've done some research, particularly on their website and in the media they (and their competitors) appear in. They say there's no such thing as a silly question, but if you ask a question that a quick search on Google can answer, it won't help you impress them. Good questions probably fall into two categories: Those about the role (What would a typical day in the role look like? What will I be expected to do in my first week/month/year? What development opportunities will I have? Which clients will I work on?) and those about the company (What are the company's growth plans? What are main challenges facing the company? How are you trying to build/alter the company's media profile?) or the agency (What business has the agency won recently? How do you see the agency growing? Which journalists do you speak to regularly?)."

Ian Burge, Senior Account Manager, Cognito, @IanBurgePR

Chapter 25: Discussing salary

If you are in the final stages of the interview process for a new job the issue of money is likely to come up. This can be a particularly difficult discussion if it's your first job and there has been little or no indication what the company is prepared to pay. Quite often entry-level roles are advertised as £competitive or £negotiable. What does that actually mean? It means the company probably has a salary range in mind, and doesn't want to restrict applications by putting a figure on the role. Currently, entry-level PR roles can pay anything from £14k - £25k depending on the sector and discipline so it's a good idea to have a look at plenty of job adverts to get an idea of the salaries in the sector you're interviewing for. As a rule of thumb, the more glamorous the sector (celebrities, fashion, beauty, music, entertainment) the less it will pay and the more serious the sector (healthcare, financial, corporate) the higher the chance of a more substantial salary.

If you are already working you have your current salary as a starting point, though most people would want to increase their income by moving jobs, especially if you are moving up the hierarchy in some way.

If that's the case, think about what your salary should be and why. Do you know anyone in a similar job elsewhere? Ask them for a ballpark figure on what this job should pay. Otherwise, scour job ads – online and in the papers – to see what is being offered elsewhere for this sort of role.

Think about your living costs – rent of course (will you have to move?), new clothes (are you moving from a casual dress company to a business dress company?) and consider your commute (will you need a more expensive travel card?). Then, when you are asked about money, you will be well prepared to articulate what you are hoping to be paid, and to justify it.

Don't forget the other benefits other than money. Private health insurance, share options, gym membership, staff canteen, interest-free season ticket loan, etc. Make a list of what you currently get, and compare that with what's on offer at your potential new company. If there is more on offer, perhaps that compensates for a less than perfect salary increase?

Most importantly, before the meeting, ask yourself honestly how much you want this job and what salary are you prepared to accept – and what you can live on. You might consider a lower increase, or even a lower salary, in return for a great opportunity to learn a lot – especially if the job has prospects.

Remember that many companies are especially cautious about pay when they first hire someone. If you do accept less than you feel you deserve – or need – ask whether you could have a salary review after your probation period, which is generally three months. Suggest that if you work hard and they are happy, then they might give you a rise

Part 4: Once you've got the job

Hurrah! You've got a job in PR. Well done you! Now for the bad news; keeping it is just as hard as getting it.

Many graduates fail to grasp that once they've got through the interview stage and got their foot in the door of a company, it's not time to sit back and put their feet up. The hard work is really only just beginning.

Working life can be a real shock when you've spent nearly fifteen years or more in education. This is particularly true if you've spent your entire educational career being top of the class and regularly praised by your teachers and tutors. Suddenly, you're the bottom of the pile; the most junior person in the company, and no one gives you much attention.

Employers often complain that entry-level PRs don't know how to behave appropriately, as though you should instinctively know how to be a professional working person. In my experience, no one knows that stuff instinctively. Some people are very lucky that they come from backgrounds where their parents work in very professional environments and so they learn from their behaviour. Some students happen to have extremely supportive careers and employability departments at school and university and the more enlightened educational institutions are doing more to make sure their alumni are well prepared for the world of work. Sadly though, that is not always the case, and most people learn by trial and error. I would hope that you make most of your mistakes during work experience and internships, before you go on to be in a permanent role. For the vast majority of PR internships the value is in learning what a PR environment is like to work in, and how other PR professionals behave rather than in actually practising PR tasks. So if your internships have mostly consisted of making tea and picking up the MD's dry cleaning you shouldn't write it off as a completely useless experience, instead think about all the work behaviours, learned while you were there, that are just as important to a PR employer – turning up on time, submitting work to deadlines, being polite.

These may seem like very obvious things, but time and time again entry-level PRs fail to impress with their work etiquette.

Beyond giving you tips on how to make a good impression, I also wanted to prepare you for some other aspects of working life; flexible working, taking a career break, going freelance, asking for a pay rise, dealing with difficult colleagues and how to resign. These are all subjects I get asked about by graduates I have previously trained, and I suspect there are many other entry-level PRs who have the same concerns but who are reluctant to ask anyone about them. I hope these final chapters help you too.

Chapter 26: How to make a good first impression

Four times a year a new batch of PR trainees join us at the Taylor Bennett Foundation. On their first day they arrive bright and breezy, and ready for ten weeks of work-based training.

The first day of our traineeship programmes are always intense and there's a lot of information for them to take in, but it's also a really great opportunity for us to form our first impressions of them. Each group of trainees we take is different, and it's a very steep learning curve for those who have very little work experience.

So, for those of you about to embark on your first day in a new job, here are my five top tips on making a good first impression on an employer.

- **Turn up on time.** If you're not sure where you're meant to be going, then do a trial run the day before to make sure you know where the building is. Being late is never a good start. Similarly, don't turn up ages in advance. It may be that your colleagues and manager have planned to do other things before your arrival, so by being early you're putting pressure on them to stop what they're doing and concentrate on you. If you turn up early, go and have a coffee somewhere nearby.
- **Wear a smile.** Even if you are incredibly nervous - and let's face it, you probably will be - seeming cheerful and friendly will go a long way to making you approachable. Being shy can make you seem aloof and cold, and that's not how you want people to think of you on your first day is it?
- **Be helpful.** If you can see someone is struggling with a task, ask if you can help. Offer to make a round of teas and coffees – everyone likes someone who will pitch in.
- **Ask questions.** If you don't ask when you don't understand something, you'll make a mistake. Better to

clarify anything you're not clear on to start with, to avoid any embarrassing errors.

- **Be interested.** Being keen is not just for interviews, once you've got the job you've got to keep it up. Take an interest in your colleagues, make sure you read relevant publications, and join in when asked for suggestions.

"Start as you mean to go on. Be enthusiastic, work hard, never stop learning. Be confident but don't be cocky – and be yourself too. That first impression really will count, and will help you launch your career. My top tips are – volunteer to get involved in things, even if you think they are 'not you' – you'll learn a lot; watch your peers and see what makes them successful, or not as the case may be; if you have a good idea, don't be afraid to speak up; don't expect to be doing all the glamorous stuff right at the start – you have to put a bit of time in first and learn a few tools of the trade; and try to look tidy and clean – whatever the office dress code . Finally have fun!"
Victoria Brough, Group Communcations Director, London Stock Exchange Group

"Top five tips:

1. Always be enthusiastic even if the task is dull.

2. Always volunteer if an email gets sent out requesting help or information.

3. Always introduce yourself to people – don't just sit at your desk and wait for people to come to you (appreciate this is often hard and requires a deep breath!)

4. Always dress appropriately and in a way that is in line with your colleagues and the tone of the office.

5. Never complain (at least, don't let your boss hear you!)"
Lucie Harper, Executive Vice President, Weber Shandwick London

"If you don't understand a task you have been asked to do then shout. Don't worry about it and then think it may just drop off your to do list. It won't. It will turn into an elephant and come back to bite you. Be quick to learn but also quick to ask advice, take guidance and learn from others. A junior PR who shows initiative and willingness to learn from others will progress.

Read as many newspapers and magazines and watch the widest variety of television programmes as possible. I find it extraordinary the number of junior PRs I have worked with who don't realise the value of reading all sections of the weekend papers to garner ideas, to keep ahead of culture and trends and actually see and understand what makes the news. If you are in the newsagent or railway station then take the opportunity to buy a magazine you wouldn't normally read. Get familiar with similar and complementary brands, with opinion writers, with lifestyle journalists and with today's news agenda. Keep a notepad on you and jot down ideas which may be relevant to your company or client. I can't stress this strongly enough."

Michele Andjel, Head of Public Relations, Carnival UK, @micheleandjel

"Follow these 10 unspoken common sense rules of the workplace:

Attentiveness

Listen and at least appear to be enthralled and engaged, even if you aren't, e.g., no texting, doodling, picking of body parts when someone else (client or colleague is talking) or during conference calls.

Be proactive

Make suggestions, come up with new ideas and share interesting information. People will be impressed if you demonstrate your interest, curiosity and knowledge. If you think you can contribute to something, volunteer. People will appreciate your can-do attitude.

No headphones

You will learn a lot from listening to and engaging with those around you. Don't cut yourself off by wearing headphones (even if others do) as you might appear unapproachable or disengaged.

Email etiquette

Work email is a formal method of communication and should be respected. Consider whether it is the best form of communication – it might be preferable to speak to someone face to face or by 'phone. Ensure that the subject of the email is accurate, double check spellings, don't cc people unless absolutely relevant and certainly not by mistake.

Meeting etiquette

Never be late for meetings or expect someone to come and remind you that a meeting is about to start. Tardiness will wind people up. If you accept a meeting invitation, make sure you attend. Be attentive and take notes and, most of all participate – make your presence worthwhile.

Never be fooled

Into thinking that your clients are your friends - they may well be friendly and share all sorts of personal and irrelevant information with you but they are paying for your professional services. This may seem like an unequal relationship. It is! Always maintain professional standards when communicating with them, even in social circumstances such as drinks.

Respect authority

Even if you don't respect those in authority, act like you do. Accept constructive feedback – colleagues are invested in your development and feedback is based on knowledge or previous experience.

Don't fake it

If you don't know the answer to a question, offer to find out, don't blag it.

Stick to deadlines

Always stick to deadlines and if you are in danger of missing them, flag this up in advance.

Accuracy is important

Don't rely on others to proof read your work - typos and mistakes will make you appear uncaring and stupid. The devil is in the detail."

Antonia Betts, Managing Director, Ogilvy Health PR, @AntoniaBetts

Chapter 27: Twenty five don'ts

Want to know how to avoid winding up your colleagues? Discover your irritating habits and make work life easier for everyone. Here's my quick and easy guide to what not to do:

1. Don't eat smelly food in the office.
2. Don't shout into your phone.
3. Don't worry about other people's time keeping. Make sure you get to work and meetings on time, let other people's bosses worry about them getting there.
4. Don't use your phone in meetings.
5. Don't take credit for other people's work.
6. Don't come into the office when you're sick, spreading your germs won't make you popular.
7. Don't blame others for your mistakes.
8. Don't sit on a task all day then ask a member of your team to do it five minutes before the end of the day.
9. If you've set a deadline for a piece of work, don't ask for it repeatedly BEFORE the deadline. What's the point of a deadline if you're going to nag for it earlier anyway?
10. Don't miss a deadline.
11. Don't interrupt. Give others a chance to speak. Don't speak over other people or ignore them completely. You may like the sound of your own voice but your colleagues will find it pretty grating.
12. Don't use endless management speak. Thinking outside the box is SO last year.
13. Don't allow your parents, friends or partner to call you endlessly at work – particularly if you work in an office where there are no direct lines. It's irritating having to take messages from your husband every fifteen minutes.
14. Don't be consistently late. A one off is a one off – everyone oversleeps or gets stuck on a defective train now and then. But five minutes late EVERY morning is disrespectful and annoying.
15. Don't shout across the office at people.
16. Don't belittle colleagues and if you have to tell someone in your team off, do it in private.

17. Don't talk on the phone with your mouth full of food.
18. Don't expect other people to make you cups of coffee if you're not willing to return the favour.
19. Don't leave the printer jammed with paper for someone else to sort out.
20. Don't put the empty milk carton back in the fridge.
21. Don't say you understand something when you don't.
22. Don't expect everyone to drop what they're doing to do something for you, unless it's an absolute emergency (and then be nice about it).
23. Don't make a mess in the staff kitchen and leave it for someone else to tidy up.
24. Don't leave the toilet roll holder empty.
25. Don't send unnecessary emails. Pick up the phone, or talk face-to-face, once in a while.

"Keep your counsel. Don't be indiscreet and don't judge people on first impressions. As you climb the career ladder you will realise the value of discretion, both with your colleagues and with journalists. You don't want to get a reputation for gossiping and never discuss what could be confidential information to your colleagues, family and friends. The ability to be trusted is key in a PR environment."

Michele Andjel, Head of Public Relations, Carnival UK, @micheleandjel

Chapter 28: What to expect in your first twelve months

Just as graduates are dismayed when I tell them no one cares about the individual modules they studied at university they are similarly disheartened when they learn what's in store for their first twelve months in a PR role.

At the end of this chapter you will hear from lots of junior PR people who will give you an insight into the day-to-day life of their job. Each job – and title – is slightly different, but one aspect remains constant throughout – administration.

You've just spent three years (or more) at university getting top grades, writing insightful essays and preparing yourself to be a trusted adviser, and then you get your first job and you spend the first twelve months compiling media clippings. You're disappointed. You're better than this, surely? The truth is this: in time you *will* become a trusted adviser, but first you have to earn your stripes. Your first year is your opportunity to show that you can just get on with a job without needing help every five minutes. It's your chance to show that no matter how dull and monotonous a task is you can do it really, really well. And a year out of a whole lifetime of working isn't very long. So my advice is to suck it up and get on with it. No one likes working with a whinger.

If you think once you get past the first twelve months your days of admin are over you can think again. You have a working lifetime of filling in timesheets and writing client reports ahead of you. Every job has a boring bit that no one likes doing and in PR this is it. So your first year is good preparation for that.

You should also be using your first year to suck up as much information and experience as you can. Now is the time to ask questions; after the first year your colleagues will wonder why you still haven't grasped what's going on.

Because there are so many PR sectors and disciplines, and because every job is so different, it's impossible for me to say what a typical day is like for a junior PR. A day at one company will be completely different to a day at another. However, to give you a rough idea, your first twelve months is likely to include tasks such as media monitoring and compiling clippings, media lists, media research, new business research, features research (there's a lot of research in junior roles) and drafting content for press releases and client reports. You may also be required to attend events to help with logistics, rather than to manage them, and it's very likely that you will be involved in team meetings and brainstorming.

I can also tell you what you definitely won't be doing. You won't be spearheading strategic campaigns and you won't be managing any crises. Any entry-level PR who has ambitions to be doing those things in their first year is misguided at best and delusional at worst. You must learn to walk before you can run.

Your first year is your opportunity to prove yourself. Sometimes this means you'll be doing things which you may think are pointless but you must grasp those tasks with both hands and do them to the best of your abilities.

Think back to the chapter on which skills PR employers value. If you demonstrated during the application process that you have all those skills, now is the time to put them to the test. Be organised, meet deadlines, be punctual, be well presented, be proactive, think ahead, build relationships with colleagues and journalists, work hard, be reliable and most of all, be likeable.

"In the first twelve months you will need to be a sponge taking in vast amounts of new information. Some days will be spent building media lists, and be utterly tedious. Other days you will be out with celebrities at events. Most of the time you will be supporting account teams working on a range of accounts. This is where your flexibility comes in. One day you might be selling stories on the phone and working on social media campaigns, the next day you're taking minutes in meetings and setting up conference calls or ordering refreshments for a big event. And you'll constantly have your writing criticised. If you don't know how to do a task, ask for assistance. If the company needs extra help, jump in, even if it's out of your comfort zone. Make yourself indispensable, and be prepared to work harder than you have ever done in your life."

Di Burton, Managing Director, Cicada Communications, @DiCicada

"In your first twelve months, expect to love that phone. You need to prove that you can 'sell' a story and make news, again and again. Don't be afraid to pitch in with creative ideas in brainstorms, right from the start, but NB – your bosses will be looking for strategic ideas. Get obsessed with your clients, learn all about the brand's journey. Be known for being the early bird. Be known for being efficient. But most of all, be known for getting that coverage. That's what it's all about. And also – enjoy yourself. It's quite exciting to be surrounded by people who love what you do, and are best at what you're best at. You may just make some friends for life along the way."

Jo Burkill, PR Manager, the Timewise Foundation, @joburkill

"I work for a small charity so my role as Head of PR & Communication is very full on. My day begins the minute I pick up my phone (which is as soon as my eyes open). It begins by checking the charity's Twitter and Facebook, and skimming through the news online including any Google new alerts, for potential news stories. I then check my emails while on the way to the office. Once I get into the office I schedule messages, images or videos to post on the charity's Facebook and Twitter pages via Hootsuite; this normally takes thirty minutes depending on what the charity's focus is for the week. And then I go back to responding to emails. Each day varies; some days I will be drafting news stories to go up on the website, attending meetings or planning fundraising events – sometimes all three in one day! If you are looking for an example of what to expect in your first twelve months watch 'The Devil Wears Prada'. Your role will be heavily admin based. Expect to carry out tasks such as creating media lists, cropping and mounting coverage, researching, booking couriers, managing stock and a lot of calling around. It sounds boring, and you may want to quit, change your sector, or leave the PR industry all together; however, from personal experience, I can say that it is important for your career to stick it out, and learn the basics. Do not expect go to events, get loads of freebies, or to post images of yourself with celebs on Instagram. As Drake says, "started from the bottom, now we're here"."

Whitney Brown, Head of PR & Communication, DiversityInCare Ltd, @_whitneybrown

"My day at work starts off with monitoring the media from the moment my eyes open (literally). I check Twitter on my phone and see what is trending, listen to the radio as I am getting ready and scan through at least two or three papers on my way to work (thank god for apps)!

Once I am in the office I answer queries from journalists as a top priority, and then plan how to angle stories for the press. As I work in-house for a skincare brand I have to find ways to make a product sound exclusive, new and exciting, even if the publication has used it before. This is why monitoring the news everyday is so important, to keep your angles current. One of the best aspects of my role is meeting members of the press face-to-face. It's always better to establish a relationship in person as the journalist will remember you better. I very rarely get cut off on the phone by people I've charmed over breakfast!

After interning for almost a whole academic year after graduating I got my first break at a boutique beauty PR agency. I worked there for six months before the recession affected the company and I was made redundant. I jumped back on to the applications straight away and was offered a role as the in-house PR Executive for Merumaya Integrative Effective Skincare.

Tips for entry level job seekers: INTERN INTERN INTERN! In such a competitive industry, work experience is the most valuable tool you can have and without it, it's very rare that an

160

employer would consider you for an entry level role. The most successful applications I've written were creative ones. Write a press release about yourself joining the company. Make a lot of noise on social media sites such as Twitter as it shows you are "out there"- but stay professional! Never slate any celebrity/ newspaper/ journalist on Twitter (even if it's the FT and you want to work in Fashion PR, it's just a no no in the PR world, and you never know who you will need in the future).

The first twelve months in communications aren't as glamorous as you'd expect. Expect to do the ground work- administration tasks, research, scanning, ring arounds, etc. You need to learn to walk before you can run so don't expect to be having dinner with Alexandra Schulman and air kissing Cara Delevingne at a VIP party any time soon! The advantage of working in a small company is that you can build your own contact book quickly and you can see the results of your own contributions more easily. In a bigger company you can just be a bee in a beehive."

Lekha Mohanial, PR Executive, Merumaya Integrative Effective Skincare, @LekhaCompany

"Like most Junior/Account Executives a lot of my job is a mixture of general admin work on accounts, research and some marketing. In PR, you'll find, even in your junior roles, that no one day is the same. Below is a breakdown of what a "typical" day is like for me as an Account Executive.

9.00-9.30am-Make a cup of well brewed coffee and check email inbox.

9.30am-10.00am Team meeting to catch-up on client work and priority tasks for the week.

10.00am-10.30am Quickly scan relevant news channels and publications for any client opportunities.

10.30am-12.30am-Send out invitations to various influencers for an important client event.

12.30am-1.30pm-Secure a byline opportunity for a client.

1.30pm-2.30pm-Write byline article and get it approved by the client.

2.30pm-3.30pm- Pitch byline article or press release to relevant journalists/bloggers.

3.30pm-4.30pm- Write a coverage report to client (this can be weekly or monthly depending on the client).

4.30pm-5.00pm-Reply to any unread emails.

5.00pm-5.30pm-Put together a rough list of priorities for the next day.

In the first twelve months of your PR career, you can expect to be doing the following things:

- Researching features for clients and putting together a comprehensive features list.
- Pitching in press releases and byline articles for clients.
- Organising events and getting clients into industry recognised events and awards.
- Writing press releases and articles for clients.
- Writing reports to clients.
- Admin work (it's unavoidable).
- Collaborating with creatives to think of amazing campaigns for clients.
- Occasionally attending events and drinking very nice wine."

Leke Apena, Account Executive, Battenhall, @LekeDoesThis

"In your first twelve months you can expect to be thrown completely in the deep end, to be given a lot of responsibilities, to meet a lot of people in the industry, and network a lot with journalists.

In my current role a typical day includes:

- Reporting and industry research - making clients aware of any particular positive or negative coverage that has appeared as well as ensuring that the client and the rest of the company are aware of interesting industry news, trends, events, campaigns, features, etc, that could influence or affect our clients or us as an agency. This includes a daily paper reading session.

- Developing my relationship with and understanding of the media andnetworking - liaising with media people to ensure that we have a strong relationship with them, so that we are ahead when pitching a story or inviting them to events . Maintaining this relationship also ensures that we become the "go-to" person if a media professional needs something.

- Reactive press office - handling any media enquiries and issues and ensuring that are responded to in a timely fashion.

- Proactive press office - looking for opportunities to secure positive coverage for the client.

- Assisting with any admin that is needed to help the account run smoothly

- Getting to know my clients inside out, so that I am the first point of call when senior members have questions or need assistance"

Francis Graham, Account Executive, Nelson Bostock, @francis_graham

"One of the most important things I have learned as a PR professional is to communicate. I know in our profession it seems like a superfluous thing to say, but you would be surprised how easy it is to forget to let everyone know what you're up to at all times, at any level of PR. It's easy to compartmentalise and think that what you're doing isn't important, but any part of research, media outreach and media lists are vital, vital components to the overall workings of a PR Agency. Never underestimate your role. Richard Edelman, once said that "everyone is an Account Executive" and this is true in so many ways. It isn't that you stop being an Account Executive as you move up the ladder, it's more like you accumulate more and more responsibilities on top of being an Account Executive.

Our industry means that we also have to communicate to the worldand the best way to know how to do that successfully us to know what's going on in the world , and so it follows, that the very first thing I do once I enter the office is monitor the media. In fact, it's my responsibility to distribute the papers across the team, and make sure everybody scans and notes anything noteworthy, whether in relation to clients or otherwise. It just becomes part of your daily routine... almost like brushing your teeth! You sip your morning coffee while scanning the papers, or browsing online. Keeping your ear to the ground is just part of the job. It isn't necessarily a dull task, however - if you're working for a headphone brand, it may be looking out for the hottest new DJs! If it's beauty, it may be checking out the latest competitors from the world's most glamorous brands! You just need to know what's going on at all times. It means that naturally you become more alert and attuned to the news around you, even when you're not working!

A lot of people go into PR thinking they're going to be in the thick of the creative process immediately and while this is sometimes the case, and it is great when this happens, this isn't necessarily par for the course. Within your first twelve months of PR you're more likely to do a lot of research, a lot of of media lists, media outreach and drafting press releases and client content. While creativity is important, all the aforementioned jobs are as important, as they are key in implementing the creative strategy successfully. This means, your first year of PR is key to honing your attention to detail, and getting writing skills down pat! It is also a great time to cultivate a voracious reading habit when it comes to current affairs! Once you have this foundation, everything else will be much easier to tackle as you progress in your career in communications.

Last but not least, do not be afraid to ask questions! Like I said, communication in the communications industry is key! The temptation is to think that you'll sound stupid or inadequate if you dare to question anything, but the truth is most people love to hear it! It shows that you're interested and on the ball, and most people will be happy to explain things you're confused about. No one expects you to do a good job if you don't know what you're doing!"

Bolu Babalola, PR Consultant, @BeeBabs

"My current job is quite different from the usual PR account Executive position. My post has evolved over time into a bit of a hybrid role, where I am hands-on in a lot of different areas - digital marketing, PR creative design and build - and also managing these projects as a Project Manager. The first twelve months in a comms job will probably not be quite what you imagined. You most likely will be given a lot of admin work and office maintenance duties, but work hard without complaint and you will soon find yourself taking on a lot more exciting projects to work on."

Toyosi Wilhelm, Account Executive, Holst Digital, @ToyosiWilhelm

Chapter 29: How to go freelance

There are both advantages and disadvantages to working as a freelancer. Some people like the advantages so much they choose to work as a freelancer on a permanent basis. Others only choose to work freelance in order to get a 'way in' to a certain industry or company, or to fill a gap between two full time roles.

As a freelancer you essentially work for yourself – the person who hires your services is a client rather than your boss. For them, you are a supplier rather than an employee. Some freelancers are based at their clients' offices, work normal office hours and sit alongside full-time employees, and as a result, on a day-to-day basis, their freelance status isn't obvious. However there are a number of legal differences between employees and freelancers.

Disadvantages

First, it is generally easier for companies to get rid of freelancers. When a company no longer requires the services of a freelancer, for whatever reason, they can just terminate their supplier contract. The freelancer enjoys few of the benefits that a full-time employee gets under law – in particular regarding job security. Indeed, the reason companies often take on freelancers rather than employees is because they have a temporary increase in workload. By taking on someone on a freelance basis the company can use their services while workload is high, and quickly end their contract once things are back to normal. So, freelancers are only ever assured work, and therefore an income, in the short term.

Second, a number of 'liabilities' normally taken on by an employer, sit with the freelancer when they are hired in that capacity. This is most relevant in terms of sickness and compassionate leave. As a freelancer you have no automatic rights to sick pay, or time off for funerals or family illness, and when you take days off for this reason in theory you won't be paid. Which means that coming down with the flu for a week suddenly becomes quite expensive. This may also apply if a company shuts down over Christmas – what for employees might be a two week free holiday, for a freelancer can be ten days less income.

Third, as a freelancer rather than an employee you will be asked to invoice and will be paid like other suppliers, rather than receiving a monthly pay packet at the same time as all the other employees at the company. If you are freelancing for a good company this may not make much difference, except you may be paid on a different day of the month from everyone else. However, whereas most companies will meet their payroll obligations without fail, supplier payments may sometimes be delayed for cash flow reasons. Plus, when it comes to your first payment, if you bill at the end of your first month of work, but the company has a policy of paying invoices only after twenty-eight days, you might not see your first lump of cash until two months after you joined the company.

And then there's the tax. Whereas employers pay the income tax and national insurance contributions that their employees owe the taxman, so that workers never have to worry about such things, that is not the case for freelancers. You yourself have to pay national insurance contributions and income tax on your earnings directly to the Inland Revenue – meaning that somewhere between a quarter and a half (depending on how much you're billing over all each year) of what you bill to your client will have to be passed onto the taxman at some point (freelancers normally pay NI monthly and income tax in an annual lump sum).

Aside from the challenge of remembering not to spend all the money you earn, only to be presented with a big tax bill at the end of the year, this also means you will have to register with the Inland Revenue as being self-employed and provide an annual tax return in which you declare your earnings. A tax return isn't as daunting as it probably sounds, and you don't need to be an accountant to fill it out, though a lot of

168

freelancers do pay an accountant to do it for them – which will normally set you back a few hundred quid.

Advantages

So, you have no job security, don't earn when you're ill and have to do your own tax return. What, exactly, are the benefits of being freelance?

Well, depending on your agreement with the company you freelance for, normally you have more freedom. It's more common for freelancers to work at home, to work their own hours, and to take impromptu days off than it is for employees. Freelancers can also normally work for multiple companies at the same time – providing there are enough hours in the day – so a freelance career can offer more variety too.

And there are financial benefits as well. Freelancers normally charge a higher hourly rate than employees doing the same job. Not only that, but freelancers might get away with paying less tax because they can deduct 'business expenses' from the money they earn before tax is calculated (and because tax is a percentage rate, that means less tax to pay overall).

'Business expenses' means any money you spend securing or doing your freelance work (so printing business cards, buying stationery or a new laptop for work purposes, or travelling to meetings). There are obviously rules about what you can and cannot include here, which is another reason many freelancers use an accountant to do their tax return – where these expenses are declared – because they know what you can and cannot claim. Even if you do hand all this over to a specialist, you do need to remember to keep a receipt for everything you buy which could be set off against tax.

So, to conclude: less job security and more liability, but possibly more freedom and more short-term money – which would you prefer?

I should point out that it is almost impossible to be a PR freelancer until you have a reasonable amount of experience under your belt. Employers want to hire you for your expertise and you are unlikely to have the skills and experience they need to fill a gap unless you have a decent work history behind you. So if you hanker for the freedom of freelancing, it's always wise to make sure you have some solid experience in a full time job first.

One last point

Because of the potential tax benefits enjoyed by freelancers, and the reduced liability for companies who use their services (instead of hiring employees), sometimes a firm might hire a freelancer to do what is basically a full time job – the would-be employee agrees to forego some of the security that comes with employment because of the tax breaks. Be warned though, the Inland Revenue doesn't like this, and can force companies to convert full time freelancers into employees. As a general rule freelancers should only be hired because a certain skill or general manpower is needed for a short-term project, not as an alternative to properly employing a workforce. Should a freelance contract you're being offered sound like a quasi-full time job, then it might be worth getting advice from a lawyer or accountant as to what the tax man might say.

Chapter 30: Working from home

As employers become more relaxed about flexible working practices, many more people are finding that they can work from home.

For some jobs, a phone line, laptop and internet connection is all that's needed, so the option to commute from your bedroom to your workspace instead of a long journey in a car or on a train is very appealing.

Working where you live can be beneficial for both employee and employer. If you focus, you can get more done. There are less likely to be distractions from colleagues and you can get on with the task in hand. You will spend less money – no daily breakfast coffee or sandwich from Pret, and you may save on the commute. You also get to spend more time with your family (or flatmates!).

If an average commute is two hours a day, that's ten hours a week you get to spend doing something more constructive. The bottom line is that working from home can make you more productive.

But of course it's not all sweetness and light. There are downsides too. The lines between work and home can get blurred and it can be difficult to switch off. You may also find that you get a bit lonely and there is a danger you will fall into the laziness trap. From an employer's point of view it can be frustrating if you don't feel your staff are pulling their weight at home, and that they are not instantly available for a meeting. But there are things you can do to make sure working from home works well for both you and your employer.

I work from home two days a week and my husband works from home permanently so I am very familiar with the pitfalls. Here are my tips for how to work at home effectively:

1. Have a separate work area. If at all possible, a separate room is the way to go. Somewhere where work is work, so that your home life remains separate to your job, is a good idea. In my case, my husband works in the spare bedroom and I have a desk in the living room. We don't speak for most of the day – we work for different companies and when we are working, we are working.

2. Don't turn the telly on. Ever. It is tempting. Hours of fun with 'Homes Under The Hammer' and 'This Morning' may seem like a good idea, but believe me, it's not. You may think you can work effectively with the TV on in the background, but it is a distraction. You are not a student, you are being paid to work. The radio or some quiet music is a better option.

3. Make time for lunch. We all know it's important to take breaks when you're working. Having a lunch break is a good start. It doesn't have to be a whole hour, but twenty minutes away from your computer screen is a good idea. Make sure your colleagues know when you are away from your desk and when you will be back. If you can, set your phone to do not disturb. Many people who work from home find they actually take fewer breaks than when they're in the office as they're worried their colleagues will think they're slacking, but it can really put a strain on your eyes, and your brain, if you stare at a computer screen all day so do try and take some time away.

4. Make sure your colleagues know when you are available and when you aren't. People who work from home often feel guilty and are concerned that their boss and colleagues are suspicious that they're not working hard enough, and as a result work much longer hours than they would if they were in the office. Your colleagues may not be keen on you working from home, particularly if it's not a common occurrence at your firm. They may resent the flexibility you have and be suspicious that you are actually dressed in your nightie, and sitting in front of 'Trisha' scoffing shortbread biscuits instead of actually working. Make it clear that you will be working from x o'clock to y o'clock and will be taking a half an hour for lunch at a particular time.

5. Have a decent chair. Back pain will make you unproductive and resentful.

6. If you have children, make sure you make proper arrangements for child care. Many employers now will insist that you send them to nursery or a child-minder while you are working, which is fair enough. But a few lucky people have employers that are a bit more flexible and allow them to work slightly odd hours in order to be there for their children – so they may allow you to work in the evenings instead of nine to five, for example. Whatever your arrangements, make sure your employer is aware and happy with them.

7. Get dressed. I have made this mistake. Got out of bed, read emails on my phone and then logged straight in on my laptop to start replying to messages. Before I knew it, it was lunch time and I hadn't had a shower or got dressed. Even more embarrassing is when you have to open the door to the postman still in your dressing gown. You would never go into the office in your PJs so take some time to get yourself groomed and dressed.

8. If you are sick, you are sick. Let your boss know. Turn your out of office on and go to bed.

9. Don't take advantage. Don't assume that just because you are at home you can swan off to pick the kids up from school or go to the hairdressers in the middle of the afternoon. You wouldn't do that if you were working in the office, would you? Ask your bosses permission to finish early or start late. You are still employed, just in a different environment. Of course different rules may apply if you are freelance and paid for a piece of work rather than hours worked – in that case it's up to you when you work and when you don't. If you don't finish the work, you don't get paid.

10. Use technology. Email and remote access to computers are a fantastic way to keep on top of things, but don't forget the phone. Many of us would much rather write an email than speak to someone but you could be missing a trick. Hearing a friendly voice will stave off loneliness, and help you to build relationships with your colleagues. By not being in the office, you may miss out on the banter so it's important that other people realise you are still part of the team.

"Maintaining focus while working from home can be a hard task. Getting up to make yet another cup of tea disrupts this focus and stops you getting the important work done. To help keep that focus, make a to do list of the three most important tasks you need to finish that day - and make sure you finish them. Then even if you do nothing else, you'll have completed the most important work. Other tips include turning off email and social networks for an hour, so you can concentrate on actually getting work done. Also, leave the TV switched off as it's too attention grabbing, but radio can be nice as background noise. Make sure you finish work at an appointed time in the evening, no matter what. Not only will you be more focused in order to get finished on time, but you'll also be able to relax in the evening and get a better night's sleep. You can always get up early the next day to finish off anything urgent, but your mind will be more refreshed and you'll finish the task quicker than if you plough on into the night."

Ben Matthews, Head of Communications at FutureGov and Former PR Lecturer, @benrmatthews

"Working from home is a skill in itself, and you have to be sure you know how to make the most of it. Even with flexible working patterns and many employers demonstrating more understanding of family needs, the ability to work from home for part or all of your hours is something you should respect and in turn demonstrate that it can be a huge benefit to the business. Making sure you have the right set up to work in a focussed manner is half the task; you are far more likely to do an honest day's work if your work space resembles the office rather than the kitchen table. But more importantly, having the right attitude and showing how the time away from office can allow you to work in more depth on an area such as strategy is key.

If your job involves entirely home working then be sure to set up clear boundaries of activity within your day. Whilst it is great that it gives you flexibility to do some hours outside of normal office time, ensure that your day still has a structure, and don't allow work and home life to blur across your entire waking hours. Laying ground rules and defining times for work or home life are essential to make this balance work well, and even more key in PR and Comms where being 'on-call' means the boundaries between working and not are less obvious.

Working from home is becoming more common, but for many businesses it is still early days. In PR accept that whilst you are very contactable through various means, there is still an expectation by many sources to reach people at the office and a mix of both worlds is probably the best combination."
Liz Birchall, Head of Communications, British Athletics @lbirchall

Chapter 31: Dealing with difficult colleagues

In my experience there can be two kinds of difficult colleagues; bosses and peers. Let's start with bosses.

Unfortunately, it is a fact of life that at some point in your career you will have to work with people who are particularly demanding and who you may not get along with. In general, my advice would be to suck it up for now. It won't be forever, and getting a year of solid PR experience on your CV will make you very employable in the future.

That said, there are a few things you can do to make your boss more bearable. Don't make silly mistakes. Proof read, proof read, proof read. I cannot emphasis enough how irritated bosses get with receiving releases and reports containing typos and small errors.

Do your bit. Make sure you do more than your fair share. Volunteer to help out and be proactive. Short tempers are often caused by stress so offer to relieve some of the pressure.

Take responsibility. If you make a mistake, put your hands up to it quickly and offer a solution. Denial will always make things worse.

Keep calm. Panic and tension breed panic and tension. Be the voice of reason and the person that everyone turns to in a crisis.

If all else fails - take a deep breath and count to ten.

The good thing about a difficult boss is that you learn very quickly how not to manage other people. It's a great lesson for the future, so when your time comes to manage a team, keep in mind how you felt when your first boss ranted and raved at you, and aim to be a better team leader.

More difficult to deal with than a demanding boss is a demanding colleague. You sort of expect your manager to make demands – although it would be great if they did it nicely – but colleagues who treat you like dirt are much harder to handle.

In the first instance, unless the issue is something very serious like racism or sexual harassment, you should try to resolve any issues you have with your colleagues directly, rather than going to your manager or HR with the problem. You are a grown up, this is not school or university any more, and being able to manage difficult relationships is a sign of maturity. Killing with kindness is often the way to go. It may be that your colleague is having a particularly stressful time at home and is venting their frustrations at work, so a bit of kindness might be enough for them to realise that they are acting unprofessionally.

If a subtle approach isn't working it may be that you have to tackle them head on. Ask them if you can go for a coffee out of your work environment. Take a list of points you want to raise and then calmly talk through them. Do not shout or lose your temper. It's possible that your colleague had absolutely no idea that their behaviour is impacting on you so strongly and that a sensible discussion is enough to nip the problem in the bud.

There might come a time when you feel that your direct approach hasn't worked and it's time to escalate it to your manager. If you do this, you are in danger of having an effect on your colleague's career prospects, so such a step mustn't be taken lightly. When listing your concerns keep to the facts. Cite examples of what the problem is and try to keep emotion out of the discussion with your manager. They may then try to mediate a meeting between you and your colleague so be prepared to have to face them in front of your boss. The final step in most colleague disagreements is to go to the HR department – if your firm is large enough to have one. This should be the absolute last resort, and if it gets that far you may feel you've failed to manage your work relationships successfully.

Keep in mind that generally you don't get to choose who your colleagues are as you don't hire them yourself. If you are lucky, your colleagues may become friends but it's not essential that they all think the same way that you do – and actually, in terms of building a good business, most managers do want independent thinkers with different approaches to solving problems so it's very likely that you will work with people who are very different to you. You will spend a long time in the office with them every day, so peace and harmony helps to create a nicer working environment, but you don't have to go home with them every evening so if there are minor disagreements you should be able to leave them in the office.

99% of the time you will get along with your colleagues, but it is inevitable that you will butt heads with someone at some point, and handling that in a professional manner is the key to being seen as management material.

Chapter 32: How to ask for a pay rise

Nobody likes asking for a pay rise. We hope that our efforts will be recognised and rewarded, but sadly that's not always what happens. Managers may be busy focusing on budgets and targets and sometimes you have to stand up and ask, instead of waiting for extra cash to just appear in your pay packet.

Factors to consider before you ask for a raise include:

Market information.

Consult a specialist recruiter in your field to find out what your salary band should be. Keep the whole package in mind. You may find that you are paid at the lower end of the scale for your position in the market, but then you may have a fabulous pension scheme or car allowance which compensates.

Pay scales.

Find out if there are restrictions in terms of pay scale where you work. You may find that you are already at the top of that scale and your manager is restricted as to how much they can pay you, in which case you need to find out what you would have to do to achieve a promotion and go up to the next grade.

Your cash value.

Work out how much money you have saved/earned the company in the last twelve months and ask for an increase based on your cash value to the company.

The management's point of view.

See it from the other side. How valuable are you as an employee? How easy would you be to replace? What precedents would it set for other employees?

How to approach the subject of a pay rise with your manager:

Find out when the next salary review is due.

If it's in the next few weeks you may be better off waiting until then to make your case. If it's not for another six months, request a discussion with your manager.

Ask for a face-to-face meeting.

An email will not suffice. You need to discuss the issue rationally and calmly and give both your manager and you the opportunity to ask questions.

Take with you to the meeting a list of achievements.

And reasons why you deserve a pay rise.

Also take with you evidence of your market worth.

Take along testimonials from recruiters and salary surveys stating what your skills would be worth elsewhere.

What to do if your pay rise request is declined:

It may be that your manager is restricted by current budgets.

Ask when the next pay review will be and ask if you specifically will be considered for an increase in salary.

Negotiate other benefits.

There may be no more money in the salary pot, but you may be able to negotiate a higher contribution to your pension, flexible working hours, or extra training opportunities.

Ask for extra work and responsibility.

And have achievements linked to an increase in pay.

It may be tempting to threaten to resign in the hope that your employer will try to keep you with the offer of a higher salary. This is a dangerous game to play (particularly if you don't have an offer of a job elsewhere).

Remember that you are in your career for the long haul and you want to burn as few bridges as possible. If you give your employer every opportunity to help you boost your salary and there is still no possibility of a raise or increased benefits, then perhaps it's time to start looking around for a new position elsewhere.

"If you think you deserve a pay-rise then here's a couple of recommendations on how to handle it. Firstly make sure you've done your research and looked at what the industry averages are and where you fit on the scale. Bear in mind, for example, if you are a brand new AE your salary might not be the same as an AE who has been in the job for two years. Salaries are generally based on what you merit not what you need. Secondly, don't go into your bosses' office and say you need him or her to match the offer from another agency/company or you'll leave. No-one likes being bounced, so even if you get the money, it might be to your detriment later. Much better to have a planned conversation that goes along the lines of "I want to move my pay up to around £XXX over the next year. What do I need to deliver to the business to make that happen?" Any decent boss will respond well to this and, hopefully, together you can agree a plan of action."

Giles Fraser, Co-Founder, Brands2Life, @gilesfraser

Chapter 33: Crossing sectors

A common complaint from PR practitioners is that their past experience has pigeon-holed them into a particular sector, which can be frustrating if their dream job in another sector then pops up and a recruiter refuses to consider them.

Is there anything you can do about it? Well, it depends. For those of you who are very junior, having sector specific experience shouldn't be too much of an issue. I know of Account Executives who have successfully moved from financial PR to consumer PR for example. Under eighteen months of experience and your skills are very transferable.

It may mean, however, that you have to wait a bit longer for that promotion to SAE or Account Manager while you build experience in your new domain. And you need to be able to convince recruiters that you have a passion for the sector you want to move into, and that the skills and experience you've gained so far are as relevant as if they hired someone who has a sector relevant work history.

Similarly, if you are very experienced then switching sectors is very possible too. Practitioners with ten years or more experience are often hired for their managerial abilities, crisis management experience and strategic planning skills, and so an employer may not be too concerned that you don't have specific experience in their sector.

It's those who fall in the tricky two to ten year experience bracket that are going to find making the switch hard. At this Account Manager to Associate level an employer is looking to hire someone who can hit the ground running, and that often means having a little black book of relevant journalists in the appropriate sector. There are some areas which are a bit more compatible than others, and switching from, say, fashion PR to beauty PR may not be too much of a leap. But if you want to move from fashion to tech or healthcare, you're going to have a bigger battle on your hands.

There are some things you can do to smooth the way for this transition though. If you work for a large multi-sector agency, ask to help out in your desired sector, even if it means doing a few extra hours. Getting relevant experience on your CV is going to be your golden ticket. If there's no possibility of gaining that experience in your current firm, then try volunteering to do some PR directly for a brand in that sector on a pro-bono basis in your spare time.

Start a blog which focuses on the sector you are interested in and write opinion pieces on relevant PR campaigns. Making it very visible that you have a passion for this new area is a good way to convince employers that you are serious about making the switch. Pay attention to which journalists would be key contacts and start building a relationship with them. Read their articles, follow them on Twitter and quote them in your blog posts.

You may have to be prepared to take a slight demotion in order to move to another sector, although some employers are quite enlightened and will value your transferable skills more than you may expect them to. So it may be difficult, but not impossible, to make the move to a new sector. But prepare yourself for a steep learning curve if you manage to find the job you really want, and don't expect it to be an easy ride.

"Perhaps ten years ago there was a real divide between 'corporate' and 'consumer' PR. And once you specialised in one area it seemed really difficult to cross over to the other. But that distinction is disappearing. Indeed clients are explicitly looking for agencies and individuals who are as comfortable working on one side as another. The best way to get that experience - like a lot of things in PR – is to gently muscle in on situations where you think you might learn things.

It sounds obvious, but if you're coming at things as a consumer specialist, you should always consider the reputational impact of any consumer activity before going ahead with it. Some organisations are edgy, and some are risk averse. You need to understand who you're dealing with at an early stage and plan accordingly.

Similarly, if you're already a corporate expert, one way to cross sectors is to consider how you'd adapt the same messages to a more consumer audience. In some cases this requires a radical tactical rethink, but in others the changes will be surprisingly subtle.

In either case, the way to cross sectors, in my opinion, is to always put yourself in the mindset of your target audience, and ask 'What's in it for me?' If what you're proposing is something that the person you're trying to reach is likely to pass on to their peers, then you've got it just right."

Chris Reed, Director, Fishburn Hedges and 77PR, @chris_reed

Chapter 34: Going part-time

Finding a part-time job in the PR industry, at a junior level, is almost unheard of. I'm sorry to be the bearer of bad news, but it is more than likely that you will be doing five days a week, and at least 9am – 5pm, for a fair few years. But as you gain experience and become a valued member of your team you may find that your firm is more open to the idea of you working part-time hours.

So, you've requested to go from full time to part time and your firm has agreed, hurrah! Then the little niggly worries start to set in. Will my colleagues still treat me the same? Will I still have the same chances of promotion? Have I just stalled my career?

The answer will depend on your firm, but the negative outcomes are less and less likely. The 21st century has brought with it flexible working practices and employers with an enlightened view on keeping top talent. More people than ever are going part-time, most commonly for childcare reasons, but increasingly also so they can pursue a hobby, or engage in training in a new area, or just to spend less time in the office. Employers know that time is becoming more valuable to their workforce, and in a time when a salary increase may not be possible, a reduction in working hours may be just the ticket instead.

Rather than being afraid that part-time workers will not be as engaged as their full-time counterparts, employers often soon realise that they can secure more company loyalty by allowing more flexibility, while also reducing their salary bill. And, in fact, they often find that part-time workers go above and beyond to prove that they are still as enthusiastic about their role as they ever were.

So, if employers now embrace part-time workers, and going this route can allow you time to achieve personal goals and give you more time away from the office, what are there downsides?

Inevitably, there are some. Whilst your reasons for going part time may include relieving some stress, you might find the opposite is true. Many people find that when they go from a five-days-a-week to a four-days-a-week role, they just end up doing five days of work in four days. Is that fair? Not really, but be prepared to argue the business case to your employer as to why they need to hire extra help elsewhere to relieve the strain (or at least why some tasks should be removed from your job description).

And, of course, going part time will likely also result in a drop in salary. If you're spending 20% fewer hours in the office, you may get a 20% pay cut. Ouch.

Though for lots of existing part-timers, the financial sacrifice is worth it.

Chapter 35: Taking a career break

It's become increasingly common for PR practitioners to take some time away from work, either to raise children, look after a relative or to take a sabbatical and travel the world. When you've been on a career break for a significant length of time, how should you go about re-entering the workplace?

1. When writing your CV make it clear why you've not been working recently, otherwise employers will just assume that no one has wanted to hire you.

2. Go on a training course. Brushing up on some industry skills will help boost your confidence and you can talk about it during interviews. Nothing says 'I'm keen to work' like investing in relevant training.

3. Use your contacts. If you've been clever about it, you will have stayed in touch with ex-colleagues and managers. Give them a ring and ask if they know of any vacancies. You never know, if you did a good job the first time they may be happy to hire you again.

4. Splurge on new clothes. If you've been taking the kids to school in jeans and a t-shirt, or hiking through the Amazon rain forest in shorts and a vest, you might need to revamp your wardrobe. If nothing else, you'll need at least one business-like outfit for interviews.

5. During interviews make it very clear that you are ready to return to work and fully committed to taking on a new role.

6. Don't be apologetic. You've taken time off for a very good reason. All the years you worked before your career break still count for something, so make sure you sell yourself and have a mental list of work related achievements ready for interviews.

7. Try freelancing. Firms may be more willing to take a punt on you if it's on a short-term contract, and many contracts end up going permanent anyway, so it could be your foot in the door.

8. Once you've got a job, make friends with the receptionists and admin staff. These are the people in a company who really know how things work and can smooth the return to work for you.

9. Don't say 'we used to do it another way'. Things may have moved on since you were last at work. You'll have to embrace a new way of doing things and constantly remarking that things have changed will only serve to remind everyone that you've not been in a work environment for a while.

10. Be social. Not so easy if you have childcare commitments, but try to make an effort to attend social events with colleagues occasionally. Building rapport with your teammates and managers is an important part of advancing your career.

Chapter 36: When to look for your next job

Some people stay at the same company for their entire career. It's less common than it used to be, but it does happen. Others change their jobs more often than they change their underwear. So is there a right time to move jobs, or should you be aspiring to work your way up to the very top at your current firm?

Recruiters are often nervous of interviewing people who either job hop constantly or have stayed at the same company for a very long term. The job hoppers are a risky prospect because you'll spend time and money training them, integrating them into your team and possibly paying a recruitment fee to hire them, and then they leave and you have to do it all over again. The long-termers are a risky hire for totally different reasons. If a person stays at a company for a lengthy period – say over ten years – there is a danger that they become institutionalised. They get set in their ways and it can be hard to get a leopard to change its spots. And sometimes spots need changing.

So how do you make sure you don't fall into either of these camps?

Well, to ensure you don't become a job hopper, be careful who you agree to work for. Research a company well before you apply for a job there and during the interview process make sure you are comfortable with both the role and the environment before you accept a position. Once you're in a job, you need to stick it out for a reasonable amount of time, so you want to make sure it's the right one. If you do leave a job quickly, i.e., in under twelve months, keep in mind that you'll have to be in your next role significantly longer if you want to convince future employers that you're not flighty.

If you've been at a firm for a very long term, it may be time to re-evaluate your position there. Why are you still there? Is there still room for progression? Are you still being challenged? Or are you just very comfortable? There's no reason why you have to look for a new job if you're happy where you are, but if you plan to ever make a move, don't leave it too long.

For everyone that falls between the flighty and the long-termer, deciding when to move jobs can be based on a number of factors.

Some people decide it's time to move on when it's obvious there's no room for career progression at their current firm. Others leave when they disagree with a company's new direction, or maybe a change in its ethics, or if there is a personality clash they can't resolve. Some move for money – although that is rarely the only reason.

And there are reasons specific to PR. You may decide that you are interested in a different area of the comms industry (working with different stakeholders or sectors), or that you want to move from agency to in-house, or vice versa.

Whatever your reason, before you start job hunting you should ask yourself how moving will benefit your career, and what you are hoping to get in your new role. You might also want to consider whether those things can't actually be achieved by simply altering your role within your current firm. If it's definitely the right time to leave, remember, do so with dignity and good grace, and try to leave the door open for you to return some time in the future.

Burning bridges is not a good idea in an industry as small as PR.

"PR people need to be resilient, creative and passionate. It's a tough job at times and we all have bad days. But when you no longer feel any of these things it's time to take a good look at whether you are still right for the job, and whether it's still right for you".

Nina Arnott, Head of Public Relations, Post Office, @NMEArnott

Chapter 37: How to resign

If your current boss has a severe lack of motivational and management skills and your colleagues are unhelpful, resulting in an awful atmosphere, should you mention these things when you resign?

There are two schools of thought on this. The first is that you should never burn your bridges, you never know when you might encounter these people again – what if your new firm hires one of your old colleagues? Also there is an issue of professional courtesy. News travels fast in this industry. So, say you resign and tell your boss you hate her guts. How happy is your new boss going to be, knowing that you may say the same to him one day?

The other school says you should tell the truth. It's a school Adrian Chiles now belongs to. When Chris Evans was brought in to host the Friday night edition of 'The One Show', he resigned, jumped to ITV and released a statement that he "would have been happy to stay at the BBC doing the same show on the same terms" and he was disappointed by "the Controller's decision to change an apparently successful and well-loved show at this stage". Ouch. Although it makes a change from celebrities "exploring new opportunities".

Chiles has been criticised for being childish in his approach, but some will say that brutal honesty is the way forward. How is an organisation meant to address a lack of managerial skills, if no one raises the issue? Perhaps a balance can be achieved though. Certainly raising issues is better done behind closed doors than in the public eye.

As a rule of thumb, resignation letters should be kept very short and to the point. They are not a great forum for airing grievances, and they should state the facts, briefly.

Dear John,

I am hereby giving my formal one month's notice. My last working day will be 31st December 2014.

Kind regards

Jane

That should suffice.

You may subsequently find that you are never given an opportunity to give your reasons for leaving. But most managers will want to know why, and some firms offer a formal exit interview – usually with someone other than your line manager – so that you can be more open about your reasons. This is a good opportunity to give frank and honest feedback, but do it politely and cite particular events to back up your claims. Try not to make it personal, talk about management style of the company, rather than the fact that your line manager never bothered to actually manage you.

When giving your feedback keep one thing in mind – can the organisation actually do anything to address the issue? It may help if you offer solutions rather than just give them a problem. So for example you could say "I found my colleagues really unhelpful and unfriendly, particularly when I first joined the firm and I was excluded from lunches and social events. Perhaps it would be a good idea to have long standing employees mentor new ones and take them under their wing?"

You can then move on to your next employer safe in the knowledge that not only have you got your grievances off your chest, but you may have helped to improve the environment for other employees you leave behind.

"Resign calmly, in person, followed up by a typed up letter. Try to avoid telling any co-workers in advance. Definitely no leaks to clients. Say positive things about your time in the role, both in person and in writing. Don't use it as an opportunity to vent your frustrations – it will become a permanent record. Don't expect to dictate the terms of your departure. Your employer needs to put a plan in place to deal with your departure, so be empathetic. Agree a reasonable end date, and work professionally right up to the end."

Steve McCool, Founder, Message Consultants.
@mccooltweet

"Be graceful, however difficult the circumstances. PR is a very small industry and you will cross paths again!"

Nina Arnott, Head of Public Relations, Post Office,
@NMEArnott

"It's important that you realise that you are judged by employers and peers just as much by how you leave an organisation as how you behave while you are employed. Regardless of why you are leaving, or how you have been treated, you should always depart with professional grace and elegance. It's an extremely small world and years of hard work, solid results and good impressions can be undone if you leave your erstwhile colleagues unnecessarily exposed. You should always ensure, to the best of your abilities, that you have finished off as much as you can in the time available and leave detailed status notes and useful contact information for ongoing projects. This applies regardless of how senior or junior you are. An intern who leaves like this is more likely to be asked back and or employed at a later date by an impressed colleague. Always make a point of saying goodbye to people; too many people tend to just slip out without saying anything. You should consider sending a handwritten note to those colleagues who have been particularly important, helpful or close to you. Also make the effort to say goodbye to someone you might have had a difficult relationship with – it tends to make a difference to how you are thought of in the long-run."

Brigitte Trafford, Director of Corporate Affairs, ICAP

PR recruiters

As previously mentioned, most recruitment agencies are not that keen on graduates with no experience knocking on their doors. However, once you have a solid six to twelve months of PR experience – and that includes internships – they will be much more interested in representing you. These are just some of the PR recruitment agencies you could consider registering with. Always try to go to one that you've heard good things about – personal recommendations are the best indication of whether they will do a good job. Ask them questions about what their processes are and whether they will send your CV to any employer without your permission (if the answer is yes, run a mile).

http://www.unicornjobs.com/

http://www.sgsearchandselect.com/

http://workfish.co.uk/

http://carterferris.co.uk/

http://www.majorplayers.co.uk/

http://www.prfutures.co.uk/

http://www.the-works.co.uk/

http://www.mediarecruitment.co.uk/

http://www.prospectresourcing.com/

http://www.fresh-connect.co.uk/

http://www.careermovesgroup.co.uk/

http://cloudtenrecruitment.co.uk/

http://www.premierresourcing.co.uk/

http://www.birchwoodknight.co.uk/

PR Job boards

http://www.prweekjobs.co.uk/

http://www.gorkanajobs.co.uk/jobs/pr/

http://jobs.brandrepublic.com/jobs/public-relations/

http://jobs.theguardian.com/jobs/marketing-and-pr/

http://jobs.prmoment.com/

http://www.simplymarketingjobs.co.uk/

http://www.prca.org.uk/pr-jobs

http://mediargh.com/

http://www.fashionmonitor.com/Jobs/PR-And-Marketing

http://www.ciprjobs.co.uk/

Recommended reading

PR Books

I'm often asked which are the best books on PR. There are HUNDREDS to choose from, but here are some of the best from the cheapest to the wallet crushing. Some are academic texts, some are 'guides to', one is a novel and the others are not strictly PR but are relevant nonetheless.

Why You Can't Ignore Social Media In Business by Victoria Tomlinson.

Thank you for Not Smoking by Christopher Buckley.

The Tipping Point by Malcolm Gladwell.

How to Do Everything with Podcasting by Shel Holtz and Neville Hobson.

PR Power: Inside Secrets From The World Of Spin by Amanda Barry.

Brilliant PR by Cathy Bussey.

Brand Anarchy by Steve Earl and Stephen Waddington.

Share This: The Social Media Handbook for PR Professionals by the CIPR Social Media Panel.

Share This Too by the CIPR Social Media Panel.

PR Today by Trevor Morris and Simon Goldsworthy.
Online Public Relations by David Phillips and Philip Young

Exploring Public Relations by Ralph Tench and Liz Yeomans

PR publications

PR Week
http://www.prweek.com/

Communicate Magazine
http://www.communicatemagazine.co.uk/

Corporate Comms Magazine
http://www.corpcommsmagazine.co.uk/

The Holmes Report
http://www.holmesreport.com/

PR Moment
http://www.prmoment.com/

esPResso
http://www.espressoprnews.com/

Behind the Spin
http://www.behindthespin.com/

Gorkana
http://www.gorkana.com/

PR blogs

Here are some PR blogs you should definitely take a look at:

Stuart Bruce
http://stuartbruce.biz/

Neville Hobson
http://www.nevillehobson.com/

Stephen Waddington
http://wadds.co.uk/

Stephen Davies
http://bionic.ly/

10 Yetis
http://www.10yetis.co.uk/public-relations/

Dead Dinosaur
http://deaddinosaur.co.uk/

Simon Wakeman
http://www.simonwakeman.com/

Drew Benvie
http://theblogconsultancy.typepad.com/

Sally Yates
http://www.metia.com/london/sally-yates/

Heather Yaxley
http://greenbanana.wordpress.com/

PR Conversations
http://www.prconversations.com/

Spin Sucks
http://spinsucks.com/

Sarah Stimson
http://www.stimsonsarah.com/

Useful articles

You should also be reading industry articles. Here are a few good ones to get you started:

CIPR/PRCA PR Careers Pack (free pdf download): http://www.cipr.co.uk/sites/default/files/Public_Relations_C areers_Pack_201314.pdf

Twitter Feeds for PR Wannabes:

http://spearpr.blogspot.co.uk/2011/07/top-20-twitter-feeds-for-wannabe-prs.html

Tips for getting a job in PR:

http://www.prdaily.com/Main/Articles/10418.aspx

How to get in PR and stay in it :

http://normanmonkey.wordpress.com/2012/03/20/how-to-get-into-pr-and-stay-in-it-luck-sweat-and-tears/

How to make the most of your internship

http://www.thirdyearabroad.com/work-abroad/internships-abroad/item/1074-how-to-make-the-most-of-your-foreign-internship.html

How to write a thank you letter

http://careersherpa.net/crafting-the-perfect-thank-you-letter/#.T2hXsL0Vu6c.twitter

Further contacts

The PRCA have a really useful list of PR agencies which pay their interns at least national minimum wage.

http://www.prca.org.uk/intern_campaign

The PRCA also offer student membership for £12.50 + VAT a year (free if you're on a PRCA partnership course) and graduate membership for £25 + VAT a year. You'll get access to the PRCA Student Network online, and discounted rates at PRCA student events such as their careers day.

http://www.prca.org.uk/studentmembership

The CIPR offer student membership for anyone in higher education on a twelve month+ course for £35 per year (and it's free if you're on a CIPR approved course). Benefits include a free subscription to PR Week, a work placement finder, and £700 worth of webinars and networking opportunities.

http://www.cipr.co.uk/content/membership-networking/member-grades/student

The Taylor Bennett Foundation is dedicated to addressing the need for greater diversity in the PR and communications industry. They do this by providing paid ten-week traineeships to black and minority ethnic graduates. http://www.taylorbennettfoundation.org/

There are a few Facebook groups and pages you should check out too. You'll have to forgive the unwieldy URLs, there's no good way of making them easier to read.

PR Job Watch has over 4,000 members from across the globe and regularly has PR job vacancies from UK companies. https://www.facebook.com/groups/2350659064/

PR Geeks is a group for students studying PR, and often has links to useful articles, internships and work placements. https://www.facebook.com/groups/142553755776121/

Young Black Graduates is not specifically about PR and as the title suggests, is focussed on black graduates, but they do sometimes have entry level PR vacancies posted on there and have regular careers events. https://www.facebook.com/groups/206655282748956/

PR Week ranks PR agencies annually. Check out the top 150 agencies, or pick a specific discipline (consumer, tech, healthcare, etc.) and have a look their particular table. There's also a ranking system for agencies outside of London. Always worth working your way through those agencies' websites to see if they're recruiting, and if not, send a speculative application. http://www.prweek.com/uk/go/top150/

Thank you

Thank you for reading 'How to get a job in PR'. I hope you've found it useful.

I'd love to hear your thoughts so do get in touch:

You can find me on Twitter: www.twitter.com/gooorooo

On Facebook: www.facebook.com/stimsonsarah

On LinkedIn: www.linkedin.com/in/stimsonsarah

On my blog: www.stimsonsarah.com

Or contact me by email: stimsonsarah@gmail.com

Reviews are a great way of helping other readers decide whether a book is the right one for them, so it would be hugely appreciated if you could leave your comments on Amazon.

If you'd like to receive an email alert when my next book is released, please send an email with 'subscribe' as the subject to stimsonsarah@gmail.com

- Google + FB = 2/3 online advertising
  spending in US in 2017.
- Tech giants immensely powerful
- Amazon responsible for 75% book sales
- FB + Google are not free - no cash paid
  but online activities constantly monitored so
  advertisers can tailor ads personally for them

Printed in Great Britain
by Amazon